# Improving maintenance

## a guide to reducing human error

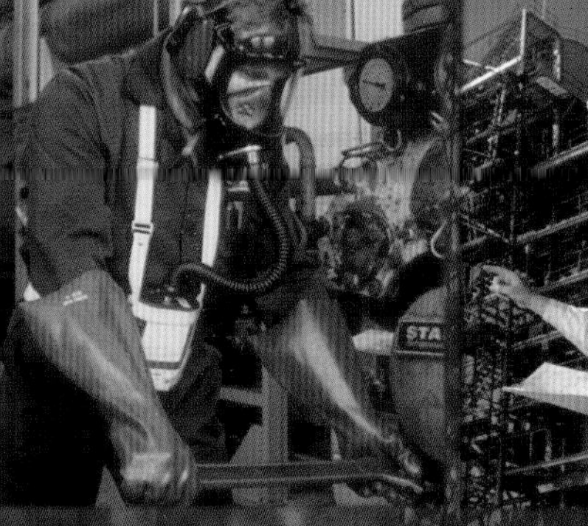

HSE BOOKS

*First published 2000*

ISBN 0 7176 1818 8



**Acknowledgements**

The authors and contributors wish to thank the supporting organisations listed above and the following people for their assistance during the drafting of this report: Sue Baker (CAA), Peter Ball (HFRG), Paul Broadaway (Atlantic Aeroengineering), Peter Buckley and John Wilkinson (Health and Safety Executive), Tony Dobson (Royal Air Force), Bill Gall (HFRG), John McGuire (HFRG), R Pearson (CAA), Eddie Rogan (British Airways) and Ian Watson (HFRG). Acknowledgement is also given to the Industry Management Committee for UK Nuclear Research Programme, HSE and the SRD Association.

# CONTENTS



CONTENTS

**HSE information sheet**

# Safe operation of miniature railways, traction engines and road vehicles

**Entertainment Sheet No 12**

## Introduction

This information sheet is aimed at model engineers operating miniature railways, miniature traction engines or miniature road vehicles as a hobby activity, either under the patronage of a club/society or as individuals. It is relevant where rides are given to the public for payment, either directly or indirectly, or, where the activity takes place in a public place. In both these cases the Health and Safety at Work etc Act 1974 (HSW Act) applies. By following this guidance you will normally be doing enough to comply with the law.

If the ride is operated in circumstances where the Act does not apply, the information below may still be helpful to operators.

Organisations which employ people or operate commercially will also need to refer to *Fairgrounds and amusement parks: Guidance on safe practice* HSG175 and other relevant guidance issued, or legislation made under the HSW Act.

This information sheet is needed because it would be too stringent to apply the fairgrounds' guidance to private clubs and societies. Operators of miniature railways, miniature traction engines or miniature road vehicles need more specific guidance. However, the fairgrounds' guidance does contain useful information on the management of health and safety by different dutyholders when the public is involved. It is suggested that you should obtain a copy for reference.

The guidance in this information sheet has been prepared after consultation with the:

- Federation of Model Engineering and Modelling Societies;
- Ground Level Gauge 5 Association;
- Midlands Federation of Model Engineering Societies;
- Northern Association of Model Engineering Societies;
- 7¼" Gauge Society;
- Society of Model and Experimental Engineers;
- Southern Federation of Model Engineering Societies;
- representatives of the model engineering press; and
- representatives of model engineering manufacturers.

It describes the application of the HSW Act to private clubs, managing health and safety, risk assessment, steps and checks for the safe operation of equipment, reporting accidents and duties when buying and selling equipment.

## Application of the HSW Act to private clubs

The Act places general duties of care on employers and the self-employed to conduct their undertakings without risk to the health and safety of others. Some of those to whom this guidance is addressed may not fall within this group of dutyholders, but their activities may create risks to themselves, those who help them on a voluntary basis and members of the public. HSE considers it good practice for those who carry out such activities to provide the same level of health and safety protection as they would if they were dutyholders under the Act.

The Act also places certain duties on any person to provide plant and equipment which is safe, so far as is reasonably practicable, for the use by other people, ie the general public, and for buying and selling.

## Managing health and safety

Health and safety can easily be achieved and effectively managed by adopting the following key stages.

### *Setting your policy*

Prepare a clear health and safety policy statement (see following example). Attach to the policy statement details of the organisation and arrangements (rules) for the health and safety of everyone involved.

> The ...........Society intends to conduct itself in such a way that there is no unacceptable risk to the health and safety of employees, members, visitors or others who may be affected.
>
> Members of the Society should realise that their acts or omissions could affect the health and safety of other people and other members of the Society. They should therefore comply with the Society's own rules and regulations.

### *Organising yourself*

If you apply a system of steps and checks for all equipment used, you will ensure that you operate safely. This information sheet contains suggested steps and checks. Individual operators need to set up similar systems to those used by clubs or societies.

### *Planning and implementation*

It is recommended that for each running session you appoint a person-in-charge who has the authority to ensure that laid-down procedures are followed. Many accidents are caused by human factors rather than by equipment failures. Ensure that everyone involved in the operation is competent, ie they have suitable knowledge and expertise for any tasks they undertake.

### *Measuring your performance*

You need to monitor your safety record on a continuous basis and particularly after any incident which has caused an accident or near miss.

### *Reviewing performance and making changes*

You need to carry out a review whenever circumstances show that it is necessary and think about what changes are needed, if any.

## Risk assessment

You should carry out a risk assessment; this is nothing more than a careful examination of what, in your activity, could cause harm to people. This then enables you to decide whether you have taken enough precautions or if you need to do more to prevent harm to people. The outcome of risk assessment is more important than the method used. The control measures which are identified by the risk assessment need to be fully documented.

You should carry out a risk assessment regularly and review it at least every three years, or sooner if modifications or new equipment change the way you operate. See the following example for guidance on the ranking of risk.

| Risk ranking | Action required |
|---|---|
| High | Take immediate action to reduce risk |
| Medium | Should be avoided - take action if possible to reduce risk |
| Low | Acceptable - but monitor the situation |
| Negligible | No action required - but don't be complacent |

## Steps and checks

### *Inspection*

One of the ways you can reduce risk is to arrange for regular inspections to be carried out by someone who is competent to advise. This person will normally be a member of the club or society concerned. In this context 'competent' means they have the knowledge and expertise in relation to the equipment concerned. These people should know their own limitations and not be expected to understand everything. If they are presented with a particular issue outside their field of knowledge they should seek the opinion of someone more suitably qualified.

These inspectors need to be of such standing, and 'independent' in their judgement, that their views are respected. 'Independent' in this respect means that they should not normally inspect their own work or anything with which they have been closely involved.

### *Construction*

It is important that all equipment that has any bearing on safety is designed and properly constructed so as to be fit for its intended purpose. Most equipment is designed to well-proven standards and established practice.

The design and construction of any equipment that departs from these established practices should be assessed to make sure that its safe operation is not impaired. It is recommended that anyone who publishes a design, checks that the design is safe. Supporting information should be available. Designs are preferably checked before manufacture.

### *Initial test/first use*

You need to ensure that models or equipment are examined and tested before they are first used. Any steam-powered model should undergo and pass an appropriate boiler testing procedure.

### *Maintenance*

Maintenance should be carried out regularly depending on usage, operating environment and where it is shown to be necessary after any incident.

### *Periodic inspection*

You need to inspect all models and equipment periodically and subject them to re-testing where appropriate. You need to record these periodic inspections. Some equipment, eg boilers, will be covered by other relevant testing procedures (see further information at end of leaflet). The frequency of inspections, like maintenance, will depend on factors such as usage, operating conditions and the environment in which the equipment is used. Older equipment may, for example, require more frequent inspection.

You should ensure that a competent person checks those parts of equipment which could affect its safe operation before any member of the public is allowed to use or ride on the equipment.

### *Keeping records*

You need to keep all inspection records for as long as practicable, to enable a complete history to be formed and to help with future risk assessments.

## Reporting accidents

You should keep an accident book to record all accident details, no matter how minor. Any accident arising from a work activity and resulting in a member of the public being taken to hospital for treatment must be reported to HSE. Try to record full details, together with names and addresses of witnesses, as soon as possible after the incident.

## Buying and selling

When models or parts are sold, by the trade or through a business, for use at work, or in a way which might affect the public, the seller has a duty of care to ensure that they are suitable for the purpose intended and that sufficient information is provided for safe operation. If the seller has no technical knowledge of an item (such as a second-hand model bought through an agent) it can be sold provided that the buyer is advised that safety improvements may be necessary to bring the item up to modern standards. This advice should be recorded in writing between the two parties concerned to avoid legal action.

Private sales of equipment between individuals not intended for use at work, or other use which in any way might affect the public, are not covered by the above requirements.

## Further reading

*Fairgrounds and amusement parks: Guidance on safe practice* HSG175 HSE Books 1997 ISBN 0 7176 1174 4

*Management of health and safety at work. Management of Health and Safety at Work Regulations 1999. Approved Code of Practice and guidance* L21 HSE Books 2000 ISBN 0 7176 2488 9

*An introduction to health and safety* HSE Books 1997 INDG259 Free leaflet

*Five steps to risk assessment* HSE Books 1998 INDG163(rev) Free leaflet; also available in priced packs, ISBN 0 7176 1565 0

*Managing health and safety: Five steps to success* HSE Books 1998 INDG275 Free leaflet

*Passenger carrying miniature railways: Guidance on safe practice* Due to be published spring 2001

## Further information

Boiler testing procedures are available from the secretaries of the following organisations, namely the:

- Midland Federation of Model Engineering Societies;
- Model Steam Road Vehicle Society;
- Northern Association of Model Engineers;
- 7¼" Gauge Society: and
- Southern Federation of Model Engineering Societies.

While every effort has been made to ensure the accuracy of the references listed in this publication, their future availability cannot be guaranteed.

HSE priced and free publications are available from HSE Books, PO Box 1999, Sudbury, Suffolk CO10 2WA. Tel: 01787 881165 Fax: 01787 313995. Website: www.hsebooks.co.uk

HSE priced publications are also available from good booksellers.

For other enquiries ring HSE's InfoLine Tel: 08701 545500, or write to HSE's Information Centre, Broad Lane, Sheffield S3 7HQ. Website: www.hse.gov.uk

This leaflet contains notes on good practice which are not compulsory but which you may find helpful in considering what you need to do.

Printed and published by the Health and Safety Executive 5/00 ETIS12 C300

# FOREWORD

HSE has worked closely with HFRG as part of the working group which produced this guidance. HFRG has a very broad hazardous industries' representation including the chemical, nuclear, aviation and offshore sectors.

Although written primarily for the major hazard industries, the guidance addresses a topic which is important to all industrial sectors and sizes of business. Clearly though, in major hazard industries or the public transport sector the risks from failure may be higher both for business and society.

Overall, the general accident trend in the United Kingdom (UK) is downwards but the role of maintenance error as a root or major contributory cause to major accidents has increased. We have seen many examples, in the UK and worldwide, eg the disasters at Piper Alpha, Bhopal, and Clapham Junction and more recently in a number of high-profile aviation accidents.

Traditional approaches to safety have focused on engineering and process risks, and have sought hardware solutions to them. However, studies show that human factors contribute to up to 80% of workplace accidents and incidents. HSE is actively tackling this area by developing its own human factors guidance and expertise, and applying it directly in its inspection and enforcement activities.

The key message of the guidance is that human error in maintenance is largely predictable and therefore can be identified and managed. HSE expects to see industry tackle maintenance risks in a structured and proactive way, making it part of every company's safety management system. HSE is committed to pursuing the continued reduction of accidents resulting from maintenance activities, through advice and, where necessary, enforcement.

This guidance can help you move towards that goal. When applied, it will help significantly reduce accidents resulting from human error in maintenance. Furthermore, improvements in the reliability of maintenance will have business benefits beyond health and safety. I commend the guidance to you.

**Dr Paul Davies**
Chief Scientist and Head of HSE's Hazardous Installations Directorate

# INTRODUCTION

1 This guidance has been written for managers, engineers and others, such as supervisors, team leaders and health and safety personnel, who are:

- responsible for, or involved in, the management of maintenance within their organisation; and
- who are concerned with the performance of people undertaking maintenance activities.

The guidance is designed to be used in organisations of all sizes, and should particularly benefit small and medium-sized enterprises (SMEs) whose in-house resources may be limited.

2 The quality of maintenance is a major contributory factor affecting safety and operational costs. It affects the operating life of plant and also the risk of accidents during or following maintenance. The possibility of a fatal accident is present in many maintenance activities across all industries and continues to account for a large number of avoidable workplace deaths each year. However, the scale of accidents can be much larger in major hazard industries and the public transport sector (eg railways) and can affect the public as well as employees.

3 The focus on human error comes from the recognition that maintenance is largely a human activity. Although it is never possible to totally eliminate human error, it is possible, through good maintenance management and an understanding of the issues that affect error, to move towards this goal and to control the likelihood of error.

4 The guidance provides practical advice and tools for improving the quality of maintenance activities through the reduction of human error. It enables maintenance managers and others to:

- identify those issues that most adversely affect the performance of maintenance staff;
- identify the particular maintenance activities in their organisation that are most at risk from human failure;
- support risk assessments to ensure all reasonably practicable health and safety measures are taken; and
- develop cost-effective measures to address identified areas for improvement.

5 The method described in this guidance has been developed for in-house use by organisations and as such the analysis forms can be freely copied for internal use. The formats may be modified to suit particular needs but they should still contain the

reference to HSE. They are not intended for use in consultancy services to third parties. (See copyright details on page ii)

6 The information about maintenance management issues and possible remedial measures will also assist a manager who is setting up a new maintenance organisation. However, the assessment process is intended only for use on existing maintenance activities, where performance information is already available.

**How to use this guide**

7 This guide has four sections:

- Maintenance risks;
- Human performance in maintenance;
- Assessment method; and
- Maintenance management issues.

The intention is to provide a set of information structured according to the needs of the individual reader.

8 The first two sections, *Maintenance risks* and *Human performance in maintenance* provide an overview of the importance of human factors in maintenance and list the main issues that management control. These are structured according to the general principles outlined in the Health and Safety Executive (HSE) publication *Successful health and safety management.*[1]

9 The third section, *Assessment method*, provides a method for identifying the key issues adversely affecting maintenance in your organisation. The fourth, *Maintenance management issues*, provides an introduction to and guidance on addressing each of the identified issues. This final section can also be used to find further information about the general issues, without having undertaken the assessment process in the third.

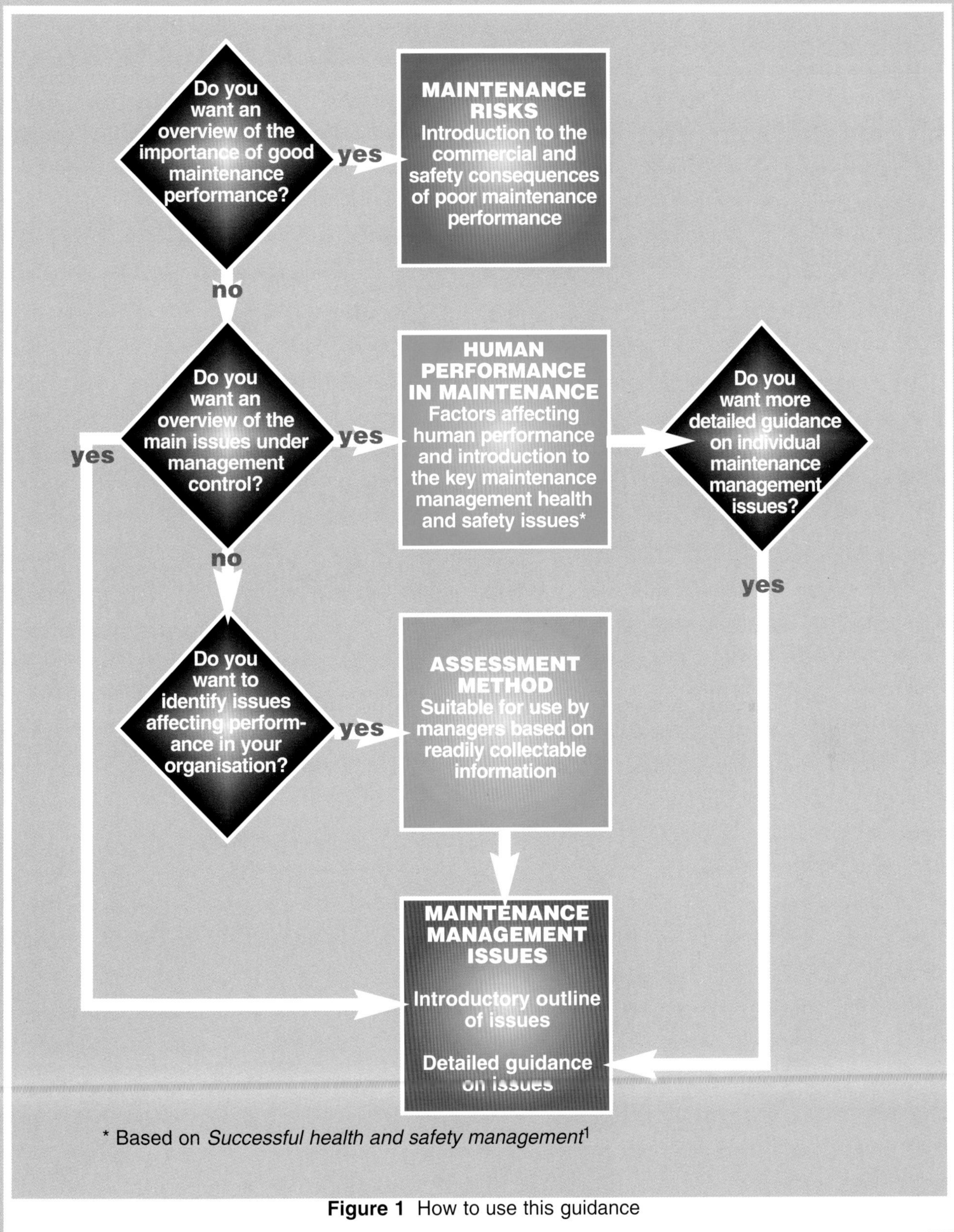


* Based on *Successful health and safety management*[1]

**Figure 1** How to use this guidance

# MAINTENANCE RISKS

*A nine-year-old boy was killed when a water-chute car at a fairground ran into a metal archway that had fallen onto the track. The archway had just been repaired.*

## Importance of good maintenance performance

10 Most items of plant and equipment rely on maintenance during their operating life. This requirement is increasingly being recognised as an important contribution to the overall *life-cost* where maintenance costs can offset any benefits of buying the cheapest item. Unnecessary costs can arise from the need for more frequent maintenance or from maintenance taking longer than necessary because equipment is difficult to maintain. A further issue relates to the quality of the maintenance work. Equipment reliability and production can be reduced, and the risk of accidents increased (during or following maintenance), if maintenance work does not meet the desired standard.

11 As maintenance is heavily reliant on human activity, maintenance quality is largely dependent on the performance of maintenance staff. This increases the risk that maintenance tasks are carried out incorrectly, particularly for complex items, where the need for quality maintenance can be very important. Although it is never possible to eliminate human error totally, it is possible through good maintenance management to move towards this goal. In addition, when the maintenance is costly or difficult to carry out, there is a greater risk that it will not be carried out as often as it should or that it will not be done to the desired standard. This increases the chance of the item failing in service, often with costly consequences. Such concerns have fuelled interest in the concept of maintainability. However, it is still common to find little regard given to this concept at the design stage of the item.

*An airline was fined £150 000 plus costs following an incident where an aircraft had to make an emergency landing following a major oil leak. The leak occurred because a maintenance fitter had not replaced the engine covers following routine maintenance. This error remained undetected when the supervising engineer failed to test run the engines as required by the maintenance procedures. Had the aircrew not reacted quickly, the aircraft could have crashed with the loss of 189 lives.*

## Safety during maintenance

12 Poor maintenance performance can have a direct effect on the health and safety of staff and contractors who carry out maintenance. The risks apply not just to full-time maintenance staff, but to any member of staff who undertakes maintenance tasks, for example office staff who replace light bulbs.

*A shop assistant in a retail warehouse received a severe electric shock while changing a fluorescent light tube with the circuit live. The company was fined £7000 plus costs.*

13 Where maintenance is carried out in an area accessible to others, there is also a direct risk to the health and safety of non-maintenance staff, for example from an electric shock from conductors exposed during maintenance. Such issues are of particular importance where members of the public are in the vicinity of maintenance activities. This is because members of the public, particularly children, will be less familiar with the hazards involved. Thus the protective measures suitable for fellow workers (such as warning signs) may not provide suitable safeguards for the public.

*A baby had her thumb sliced off while maintenance work was being carried out on a lift. Ignoring a warning sign, her parents entered the lift with the girl and descended to a lower floor. While they were leaving the lift, the lift suddenly descended injuring the baby. This was possible because the maintenance engineer had overridden the safety interlocks that prevented the lift moving with the doors open.*

### Safety during service

14 Poor maintenance performance can also lead to unreliability and equipment failures during service. In these cases, maintenance deficiencies may not be immediately evident. Of particular concern are maintenance errors that reduce the effectiveness of standby or safety equipment, as the consequences of an incident could be increased by such failures. These undetected deficiencies are often called 'latent failures'. They require particular consideration in high-hazard industries, which rely on a wide range of back-up and other equipment for safety.

*Two workers died following a massive explosion and fire at an electronics factory. A pressure release valve had been badly repaired so that it failed to operate when a tank of hot oil over-pressurised. The tank burst and the oil was ignited.*

15 The consequences of failures will range from inconvenience and loss of production to catastrophic loss of life. A tragic example of this was the Clapham Junction railway crash where the cause of the multiple fatal accident was the wiring errors made during maintenance work.[2]

16 The commercial consequences of these errors can be very high, especially in major hazard industries and the public transport sector, where the resulting loss of public confidence alone creates major long-term difficulties for operators.

### Costs of accidents during maintenance

17 Poor maintenance performance can affect both the safety and commercial performance of an organisation. For example, the tragic accident on the Piper Alpha oil platform involved a series of errors during maintenance. It resulted in the loss of 167 lives and is estimated to have cost over £2 billion, including £76 million in direct insurance payments. The extent and nature of the impact will, of course, depend upon

the type of industry and the activities carried out. A survey of maintenance activities in the motor vehicle repair industry, for example, showed that around 7000 accidents involving staff occur each year at a cost of £250 million for the industry as a whole.[3] This equates to £5000 per garage.

18 A detailed HSE study of accident costs in a range of industries has shown that they can amount to a significant proportion of overall operating costs.[4] For example, they were found to amount to 1.8% of the operating costs of a transport company and 5% of the running costs of a hospital. In addition, none of these companies experienced any serious accidents, for which costs can be very high.

***A maintenance electrician, working on top of a factory roof, fell 3.5 m through an uncovered skylight onto a concrete floor. The electrician lived but suffered a fractured spine. The company was prosecuted and fined £2000 plus costs.***

19 It is often claimed that insurance will pay for these costs. The study found that this was not the case, as the uninsured costs were typically 8 to 36 times greater than the insured costs. In addition, as the number and size of previous claims govern insurance premiums, the cost of accidents will be borne eventually in higher insurance premiums.

20 Poor maintenance performance that leads to premature equipment failures can also have significant commercial consequences even if no accident occurs. Production will often be lost. Maintenance work may need to be repeated. Additional work may also be required to correct subsequent damage to plant and equipment. Customer service quality can also be affected. In the case of motor car repairs, for example, subsequent vehicle unreliability can cause customer dissatisfaction and possible loss of business.

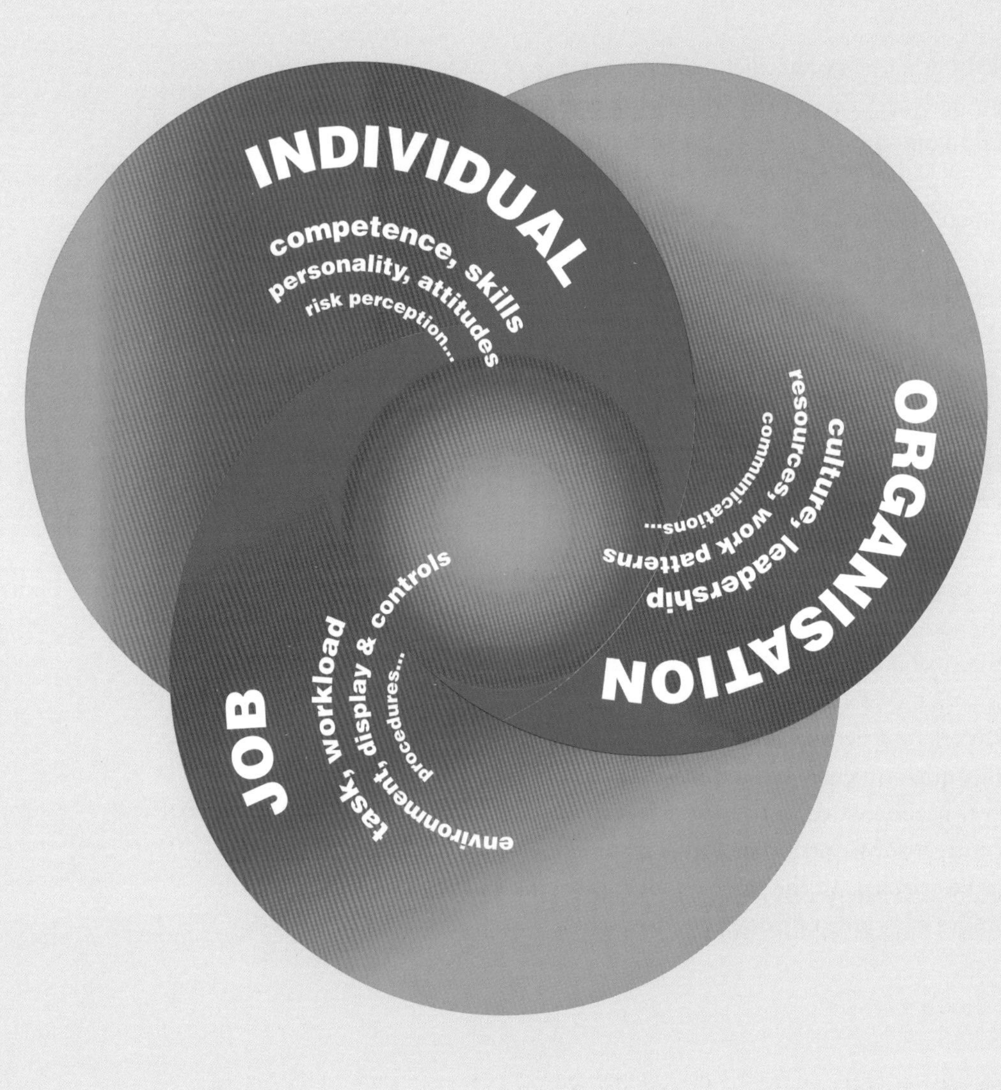


**Figure 2** Factors influencing behaviour in the workplace

# HUMAN PERFORMANCE IN MAINTENANCE

## Factors affecting human performance

21 The HSE publication *Reducing error and influencing behaviour* suggests that three overall factors affect the performance of any work activity including maintenance.[5] These human factor issues are described below and illustrated in Figure 2.

- **Individual factors:** The attributes and capabilities of the person, this includes their personal attitudes, habits and personalities as well as their skills and competence.
- **Job factors:** How the requirements of the task match the capabilities of the person undertaking the task. This includes consideration of workplace and environmental factors.
- **Organisational factors:** The organisation has a great impact on the performance of individuals, yet the importance of the health and safety culture of the organisation is often overlooked.

22 To achieve high standards of performance from staff, including maintenance personnel, these three factors need to be properly managed. This requires the maintenance organisation to have an effective safety management system. The suggested elements of such a system are illustrated in Figure 3. This is based on the HSE publication *Successful health and safety management*[1] and the British Standard on occupational health and safety management systems, BS8800.[6] These elements are consistent with those suggested for commercial management systems.[7,8]

### *Policy and organising*

23 The organisation needs to have a clear statement of policy defining its top-level goals. It should have a clearly defined organisational structure and suitable resources to ensure effective control of critical activities, co-operation and communication within the organisation and appropriate staff competence. This applies equally to maintenance as well as to operational activities.

### *Planning and implementing*

24 Maintenance work needs to be properly planned, with the associated risks assessed and minimised. The work should be adequately controlled and supervised, with progress tracked.

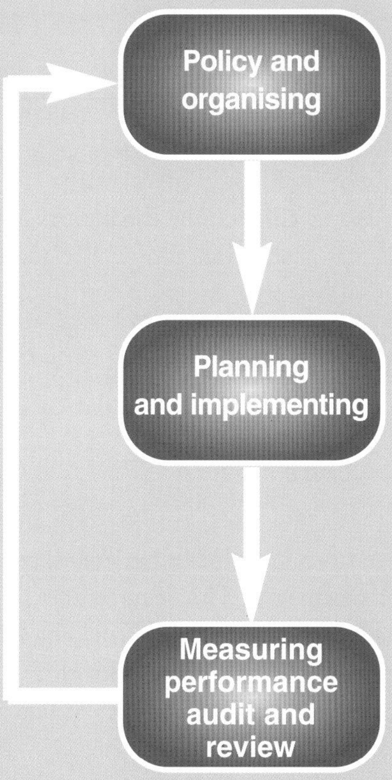


**Figure 3** Elements of health and safety management

### *Measuring performance, audit and review*

25 There needs to be an effective process of self-regulation in the organisation, supported by inspections, audits and reviews. Inspections provide for the routine monitoring of performance and workplace conditions. Audits and reviews enable a periodic assessment of the performance of the organisation to be made. Performance can be measured against the specified policy objectives and recognised internal and external standards to identify those actions necessary for continuous improvement.

## Maintenance management issues

26 Figures 2 and 3 outline the general factors involved in ensuring high standards of performance during any activity, including maintenance. Within these factors, 18 specific issues have been identified which affect maintenance performance and are important to management control. These are illustrated in Figure 4 (adopting the framework in Figure 3) and discussed in the next section, *Assessment method.* A short introduction and guidance on each issue is given in the final section, *Maintenance management issues.*

27 The assessment method described in the next section of this guidance shows how to identify which of the 18 issues warrant particular attention to improve maintenance performance. These issues should also be considered when carrying out risk assessments. An understanding of the influence of these 18 issues on the overall maintenance performance will help to identify the likelihood of human failure, and also to better assess the likely impact of various control measures to reduce the identified risks.

## Summary

28 This section outlines the main management issues governing the performance of maintenance staff. The next section, *Assessment method,* provides some practical methods to help maintenance managers identify those issues which most affect the performance of maintenance staff in their organisation. This information can then be used to identify cost-effective improvements to maintenance activities and in risk assessments of the workplace. The final section, *Maintenance management issues,* provides an introduction to and guidance on all 18 issues. It is suggested that the introductory sections are useful to give an overview of the issues and could be read separately. The related guidance sections can then be referred to for each identified issue of concern, as necessary.

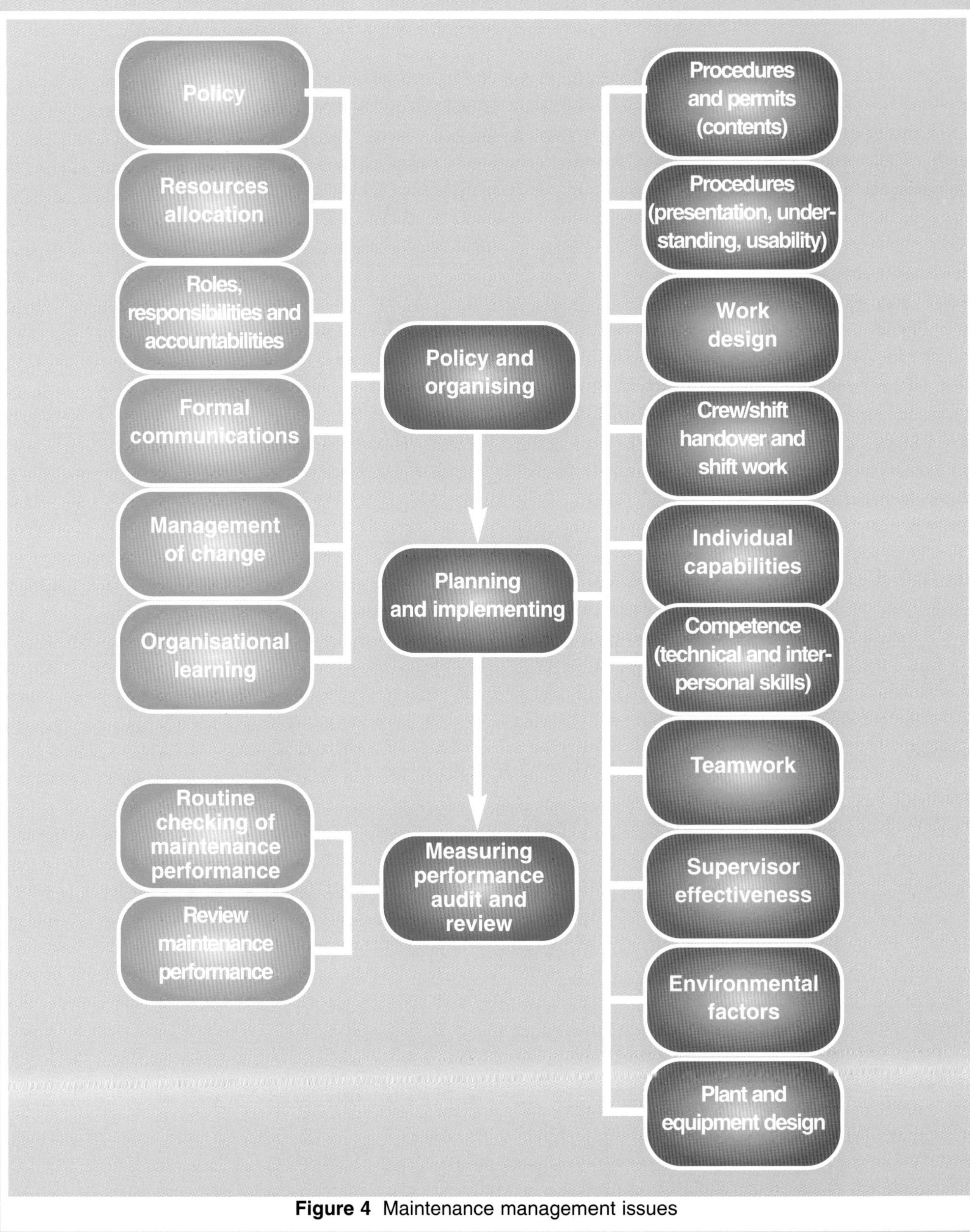


**Figure 4** Maintenance management issues

# ASSESSMENT METHOD

## Introduction

29 The previous section outlined the main issues affecting the performance of maintenance staff. This section provides a structured method to identify the relative importance of each of these issues to a specific maintenance activity or the organisation. The assessment method has three main stages, illustrated in Figure 5:

- **STAGE 1: Identification** - identify areas for assessment.
- **STAGE 2: Assessment** - assess the identified areas for the key maintenance issues of concern.
- **STAGE 3: Implementation** - prioritise areas for improvement and develop an action plan.

30 This general approach is not unique to maintenance. However, the specific methods described in this part have been developed with a clear focus on maintenance activities. There are many ways in which an assessment process could be undertaken. These methods have been chosen because they can be readily applied without specialist knowledge of human factors theory and they rely on information that can be easily and cost-effectively collected in industrial organisations both large and small.

31 The methods, in conjunction with the following guidance section, Maintenance management issues, also support the identification of suitable remedial measures. It may be useful to seek additional guidance on their implementation (see References). The overall approach is oriented towards assessing an existing organisation. Although the information in the previous section may assist a manager who is creating a new maintenance facility the assessment process has been structured for use in an established maintenance organisation.

## Stage 1: Identification

32 Where the maintenance activity is on a small scale it is reasonable to analyse the whole maintenance organisation in a single assessment. As the size of the maintenance activity increases, it is important to use this pre-assessment stage to focus on those areas and topics of most concern to the organisation, eg those associated with the majority of maintenance-related problems. The benefits of providing a focus for the assessment are twofold, namely that:

- the management issues identified by the assessment will be specific to the areas of most concern; and

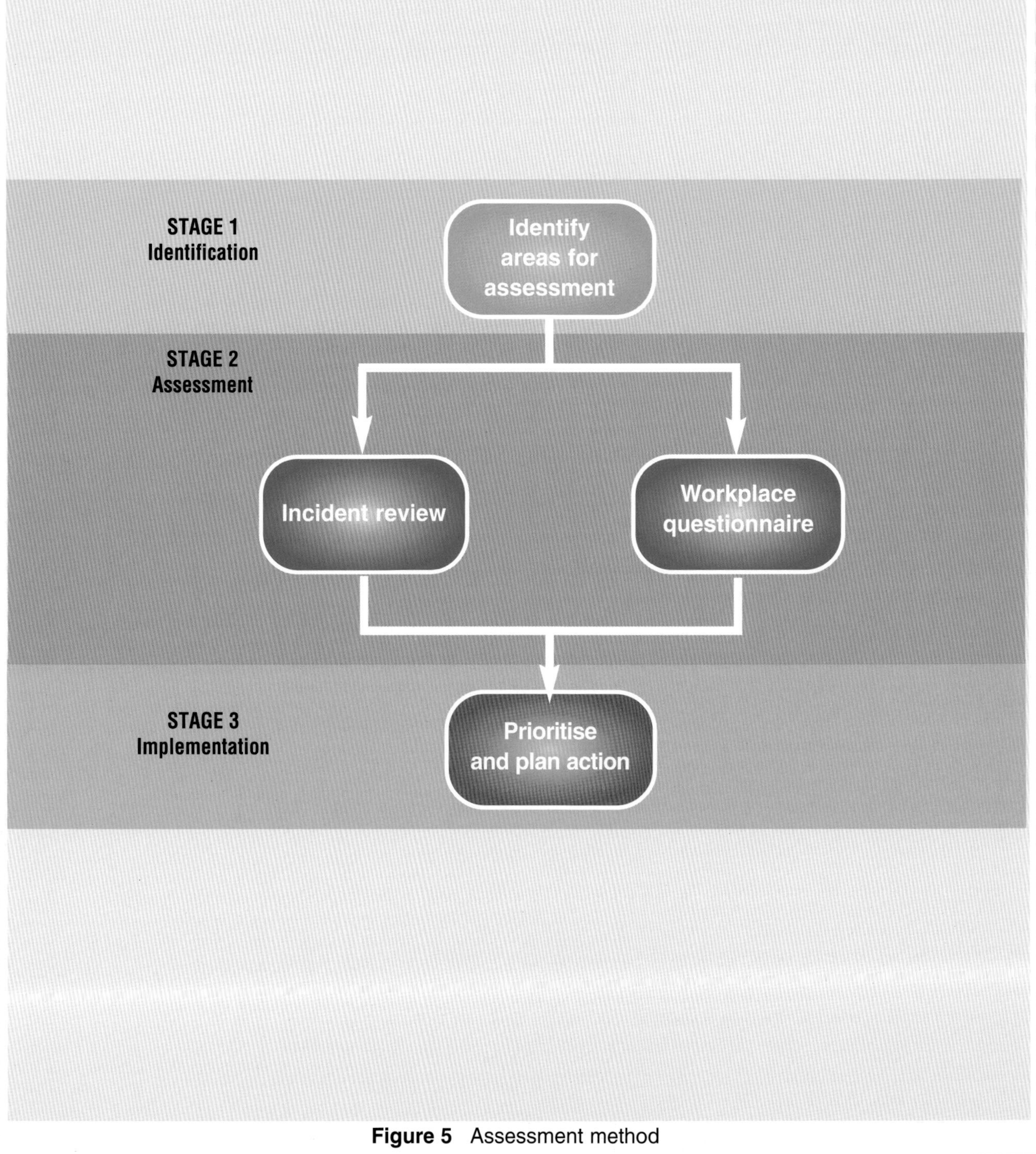


**Figure 5** Assessment method

- the assessment should be less *resource-intensive* due to the reduced scope.

33 The assessment could focus upon either:

- the factors affecting safety, equipment reliability or maintenance efficiency; or
- the factors affecting specific types of maintenance (such as those in a specific plant location, or those on a specific class of equipment).

However, there is a need to avoid restricting the scope of the assessment too far because it may be difficult to obtain enough representative data for the assessment.

34 Different ways can be used to choose which maintenance areas to focus the assessment upon. Table 1 summarises three ways, together with recommendations on which approach to use.

**Table 1** Identifying topics for assessment

| Type of approach | Ways to identify areas | Appraisal and recommendations |
|---|---|---|
| Qualitative (ie management judgement) | Use opinions of managers and/or supervisors to identify critical topics. | Warranted in small- to medium-sized organisations.<br><br>Quick and easy. But results are subjective. |
| Semi-quantitative | Use factual data, eg number of accidents, customer complaints or defect cards to identify critical topics. | Warranted in medium- to large-sized organisations.<br><br>Medium level of effort. Results reasonably objective. |
| Quantitative | Use formal hazard assessment methods (eg HAZOP*) or risk assessments to identify critical topics. | Unlikely to be warranted except in high-hazard industries.<br><br>Resource intensive and complex. But methods very systematic. |

*HAZOP = Hazard and operability studies

**Figure 6** Extract from a completed incident review score sheet

| Management issue | Underlying causes | Score 1 | Score 2 |
|---|---|---|---|
| Procedures and permits (contents) | Procedures contain technical errors | 11 | 15 |
| | Procedures contain inadequate information on task requirements | 2 | |
| | Permits-to-work not completed correctly | 0 | |
| | Errors in procedures and permits not reported | 2 | |
| Procedures (presentation/ understanding and usability) | Task misunderstood because format of procedures is poor | 7 | 29 |
| | Procedures incorrectly followed due to poor format | 2 | |
| | Procedures not used because difficult to use | 19 | |
| | Procedures not readily available at place of work | 1 | |
| Work design | Job beyond physical capability of person | 7 | 15 |
| | Job routine and repetitive causing lack of attention | 3 | |
| | Poor use of skills causing loss of competence | 5 | |
| | Excessive tiredness because of excessive overtime | 0 | |

**Score 1** = Score for each underlying cause **Score 2** = Total of scores for each management issue

42 To rank the relative importance of each management issue from the incident information, one of a number of approaches can be used. The simplest approach, and the one considered appropriate in most cases, is to record the number of incidents associated with each underlying cause. Those issues occurring most frequently are then considered to warrant most improvement. It is suggested that one score sheet is completed for each incident. The results of all the incidents used in the review are then collated onto a separate sheet. There are a number of more sophisticated approaches to scoring, described in Appendix 1, which can be used when appropriate.

43 Before starting an incident review, the assessors should be aware that incident reports often might not contain sufficient information on many of the management issues and underlying causes of interest. The assessors must therefore be prepared to either rely upon their own experience to 'read between the lines' where the documented information is insufficient for the purposes of the review, or to conduct follow-up investigations by questioning those involved to answer specific points in the checklist. In addition, the assessors may also find it difficult to decide on whether some factors are actually relevant to particular incidents. It is recommended that assessors adopt the rule of thumb that 'if in doubt' it is better to enter these factors as possible contributors. The final analysis will identify the more important and frequent entries and therefore any occasional inappropriate entries are unlikely to affect the outcome of the analysis.

44 When carrying out an incident review the assessor needs to be familiar with the maintenance operations and ideally have access to relevant staff. This enables the assessor to follow up on issues not directly covered in the formal incident investigation report. The time required to complete a single review will depend on the nature of the incident and the experience of the assessor, but a competent one may be able to review between 10 and 20 incidents a day.

***Workforce questionnaire***

45 The workforce questionnaire makes use of the perceptions of staff to identify which of the 18 maintenance management issues are relevant to the identified maintenance area of concern and so warrant improvement. The questionnaire is provided in Appendix 2 (Figure 10). The questionnaire should be answered anonymously where practicable. It asks the workforce to rate the impact that various factors have on the maintenance area of concern (as identified in Stage 1 - Identification), using a four-point scale. An extract from a completed questionnaire is shown in Figure 7.

**Figure** 7 Extract from a completed questionnaire

How much do you think the listed factors contribute to the following identified maintenance problem: *employee safety during routine maintenance?*

| **No contribution**<br>**Small contribution**<br>**Medium contribution**<br>**Major contribution** | | A | B | C | D |
|---|---|---|---|---|---|
| F | **Factor:** | A | B | C | D |
| F13 | Procedures that are needlessly too detailed or complicated | | √ | | |
| F14 | Procedures that contain technical errors | | √ | | |
| F15 | Clarity of instructions in procedures/manuals | | | √ | |
| F16 | Speed with which information can be found in procedures/manuals | | | | √ |
| F17 | Complexity of some jobs | √ | | | |
| F18 | Physical workload demands on the maintenance crews | | √ | | |

46 The number of responses (A, B, C or D) in each row from the returned questionnaires are then collated and weighted using the scale given in Table 3.

**Table 3** Weighting system for questionnaire responses

| **Questionnaire response column** | **Weighting score** |
|---|---|
| A | 0 |
| B | 1 |
| C | 4 |
| D | 9 |

47 The weighted responses from each question are collated with the aid of a questionnaire record sheet (Figure 11 provided in Appendix 2). An extract of a completed record sheet is shown in Figure 8. The relative importance for each issue is then given by the average score from the two factors associated with that issue. For example, factors 13 and 14 are both associated with the contents of procedures and permits. Note: the numbers in Figure 8 are the totals collated from a number of completed questionnaires.

**Figure 8** Extract from a completed questionnaire record sheet

| Maintenance management issue | Total score for each factor (weighted 4-point scale) | | Score for each issue (averaged score) |
|---|---|---|---|
| Procedures and permits (contents) | F13<br>35 | F14<br>39 | 37 |
| Procedures (presentation/ understanding and usability) | F15<br>74 | F16<br>82 | 78 |
| Work design | F17<br>27 | F18<br>37 | 32 |

**Stage 3: Implementation**

48 This stage involves prioritising areas for improvement. This information can be used to identify cost-effective improvements to maintenance activities using the guidance given in the next section, *Maintenance management issues.* The information can also be used in risk assessments to identify those issues requiring particular attention when assessing health and safety in the workplace.

49 The issues affecting the performance of maintenance staff are first ranked in order of priority using the assessment scores from the approach used (either the incident review or the workforce questionnaire). Appendix 3 (Figure 12) provides a blank record sheet to record the rank (or total) scores. Where both assessment approaches have been used, there may be differences in the rankings obtained from the two approaches. This is to be expected, primarily due to the differences in focus between the two approaches. Nevertheless, where these differences are significant you should recheck whether either of the approaches has been used outside its appropriate range, eg if the incident review has been used based on only a few incident reports. This can be done with the aid of Table 2 (page 16). In such cases, the results of that approach should be treated with caution and given less 'weight' than the findings of the workforce questionnaire (and vice versa when appropriate).

50 The two approaches have been designed to be complementary. The aim of the combined ranking process is therefore to identify the top three or four issues to be targeted for improvement. Using the record sheet provided in Figure 12, you can identify the top three or four issues from each approach for further consideration.

# MAINTENANCE MANAGEMENT ISSUES

51 This section provides guidance on improving each of the 18 maintenance management issues set out in Figure 4 (page 12). It is recommended that the introductory parts to each section be read initially to provide an overview of the range of improvement approaches available. Following this, you can focus on the more detailed guidance for each of those issues identified as warranting improvement. Where the incident review and/or workforce questionnaire findings show that the problems are associated with specific aspects of a particular topic, you need only consider those parts of the guidance which are relevant.

52 Care should be taken in applying the guidance since it can never be totally relevant to every situation, as factors specific to your organisation may make some ideas unworkable or inappropriate. For specialist applications, advice may be required from human factor experts. A list of professional societies who can offer this information is given in *Reducing error and influencing behaviour*.[5]

53 Further guidance on most of these issues is also available and recommended for use where the specific issue has been highlighted in the Identification stage (see paragraphs 32-34). *Successful health and safety management*[1] covers many of them (eg teamwork, supervision, management of change, and competence) as does *Reducing error and influencing behaviour*[5] (eg shiftwork/shift handover, and procedures).

**Policy**

54 The importance of developing policies covering critical business activities is increasingly recognised. However, the need for a maintenance policy is often neglected. Even where there is such a policy, it is often produced without consideration of other business objectives, eg production. Problems frequently arise when the responsibilities for maintenance are uncertain or where the maintenance policy is not compatible with the organisation's business plan. In these cases it is common for the maintenance function to have difficulties in securing adequate resources.

55 For any maintenance policy to serve a real purpose, it is necessary that staff feel they have ownership of the policy and share the views of the organisation. Problems can arise if staff, in either maintenance or non-maintenance roles, are unaware of the maintenance policy or do not accept it because they feel they have no ownership of it.

56 Every organisation should have policies covering their key business activities. One of these should cover maintenance, to ensure that the approach to maintenance is consistent with overall corporate objectives. Otherwise, it would be difficult to prioritise maintenance activities alongside competing business demands. Your maintenance policy should set out the aim of the organisation's maintenance activities and provide the framework for managing them.

*A mechanic was killed when trying to unblock a valve on a tanker. The valve had become blocked by a substance that was toxic and corrosive. During the operation, the substance splashed into the mechanic's face. The personal protective equipment provided was inadequate and allowed the substance to enter the blood stream causing death.*

***Guidance***

57 There should be clear objectives in your organisation's business plan relating to maintenance. These should outline the strategy for maintenance over the medium and possibly the longer term. The objectives, together with specific targets for the coming year, should seek to support the achievement of the maintenance policy and the organisation's other business priorities.

58 The organisation should communicate the maintenance policy and business objectives to staff to promote awareness and ownership. To aid communication, it is important that a written maintenance policy is provided to relevant parties. It is also important that senior staff visibly demonstrate their commitment to the maintenance policy, eg a manager must not be seen to place short-term production requirements before critical maintenance work.

59 All staff should be made aware of how they may contribute to achieving the organisation's maintenance objectives within the policy, eg equipment operators should be informed about the consequences of poor equipment operation on the subsequent maintenance demands.

**Resource Allocation**

60 Failure to provide sufficient resources is a contributory cause in many maintenance incidents. For maintenance the resources required will include people, time, tools and equipment, and procedures. Maintenance is vulnerable to being under-resourced, as it is not always seen to contribute directly to production targets and therefore may not receive the priority it deserves.

61 Compared with many other activities, the effects of any shortfalls may not be readily detected. Shortfalls rarely prevent maintenance activities taking place, rather they lower maintenance performance (eg by encouraging shortcuts) and the degraded output often has an indirect and delayed impact. Inadequate resources may make it more difficult to undertake a task or make the task performance less reliable. The fact that the task is eventually completed makes the detection of resource issues difficult. Maintenance staff may alter their work practices (by taking shortcuts) to overcome resource difficulties in the genuine belief that such behaviour will benefit the organisation and that it is expected of them.

***Guidance***

62 The resource requirements of maintenance must be adequately addressed including:

- personnel (numbers of staff with relevant competence);
- tools, equipment and spare parts; and

- time (ie time allocated for work and availability of plant for maintenance).

63 Arrangements should be in place so that maintenance activities can be planned to ensure that:

- resources required for each type of task are assessed and determined in advance and the required resources routinely reviewed;
- working practices are periodically reviewed and revised to reflect changing resource demands and availability;
- checks are made to ensure maintenance teams actually use the resources provided, eg careful scrutiny must be made of the opportunities and consequences of maintenance teams taking short cuts; and
- strategies are in place to cater for situations when maintenance demands exceed available resources, eg by rescheduling maintenance.

64 Ease of access to resources should be considered, such as the availability and location of tools and replacement parts. If they are not conveniently located, maintenance staff may adopt the habit of using other less appropriate tools which may be more readily at hand. They may also re-use old parts if they appear serviceable.

65 Where contract staff are used, the organisation should not assume that they have the appropriate resources to work safely. Contractors may assume that the site will provide some resources. The organisation should ensure that contractors have specified their work methods and that there is agreement on who will provide the necessary resources. The organisation should routinely audit the contractors to ensure that they do provide and use the specified resources.

**Roles, responsibilities and accountabilities**

66 In many organisations, maintenance can become undervalued by being primarily considered as an overhead with no contribution to profit. This tendency must be vigorously opposed if maintenance activities are to be successfully implemented. In particular, it is important that the maintenance programme has clearly specified roles, responsibilities and accountabilities.

67 Successful implementation of the maintenance policy requires co-operation between production and maintenance departments, and between the differing trades within the maintenance group (eg fitters and electricians). Problems can arise during maintenance if the responsibilities of maintenance staff are unclear or not well understood. Such situations are more likely to arise where maintenance staff have to interface with other groups, eg during the isolation and reinstallation of plant and equipment.

68 In addition, the responsibility for frequently performed maintenance tasks (eg cleaning and lubrication) is often not clear and this increases the likelihood that these tasks will be neglected. These situations tend to occur when no one has been given the role of co-ordinating maintenance activities within a given area, eg a maintenance engineer. They also occur when this 'co-ordinator' lacks the authority to ensure that essential maintenance is carried out, especially in the face of conflicting demands.

***Guidance***

69 There should be a clear understanding throughout your organisation as to who has overall responsibility for the maintenance programme. This programme should comprise all activities relating to servicing, overhaul, repair, inspection, testing, surveillance, etc. There should be a clearly identified group responsible for implementing the maintenance programme. This group should be responsible for both the delivery of services and the provision and allocation of necessary resources. Where maintenance is contracted out, a senior manager should be given the responsibility for ensuring that work is undertaken efficiently and safely. The manager should be accountable for ensuring satisfactory progress and that sufficient resources are provided for delivering the maintenance programme.

70 The responsibilities and structure within the maintenance group should be clearly defined, with documentation outlining required skills, job profiles, etc. In particular, the required level of authorisation for undertaking and inspecting certain tasks should be identified, and responsibility for the timing of required maintenance needs to be specified. The interface between the maintenance and operating departments also needs to be clearly defined and accepted, together with any maintenance responsibilities for the operations department.

71 It is becoming increasingly common, due to multi-skilling and downsizing, for operations staff to carry out routine maintenance activities such as surveillance monitoring, testing and minor repairs. Managers should satisfy themselves that these people have the necessary competence and resources to fulfil these requirements reliably, and that their roles and responsibilities are properly understood.

**Formal communications**

72 Maintenance frequently involves activities that need to be co-ordinated and aligned with operational demands. When maintenance accidents are analysed, poor communication is often identified as a contributory cause. Therefore, formal communications should be an essential part of maintenance management. Non-routine maintenance activities and those that span shift changeover give rise to particular communication demands. Communication channels should also encourage maintenance staff to raise potential concerns with management.

81 Changes can have an impact on staff morale and stress. These are difficult to quantify and control but can lead to a decline in performance and increased levels of absence or sickness. The effects can be managed by reducing uncertainty, increasing staff control over the changes and reducing the anxiety felt by staff about coping with the changes.

82 Uncertainty can be reduced by:

- providing clear, accurate and up-to-date information concerning the changes;
- enabling two-way communications about the changes;
- anticipating potential concerns and providing clarification; and
- minimising the period of uncertainty.

83 An individual's perception of control can be increased by:

- providing information that will allow them to evaluate the impact of change;
- involving them in key decisions; and
- providing sufficient information to enable them to start to alter their expectations.

84 Anxiety about coping with the changes can be reduced by:

- providing the necessary training and support required for new posts;
- minimising obstacles, eg from lack of authority, or financial constraints; and
- providing necessary feedback on performance in order to build confidence.

**Organisational learning**

85 The ability of an organisation to learn from its past experience is essential if the company is to successfully avoid repeating past failures and is to keep ahead of the competition. It also helps to demonstrate that the organisation has a commitment to continuous safety improvement. Maintenance activities are no different from any other activities in this respect, although they often do not receive the attention they deserve. Traditionally, maintenance units are poor in this respect. They often react to imposed changes rather than proactively seek business improvements.

86 The lack of organisational learning inhibits the effective application of corrective actions for maintenance deficiencies (including incidents). It also inhibits an organisation's opportunity for continuous improvement, so effort is required to ensure that maintenance staff are actively involved in the identification and implementation of improvements in maintenance activities.

*Guidance*

87 Your organisation should promote a culture of continuous improvement. It should put in place systems to encourage staff to identify improvements to maintenance practices so that the organisation can assess them for suitability. Such systems will encourage the involvement of staff in maintenance improvement, which they should find rewarding. In particular, your organisation should have:

- clear goals, strategies and plans for improving maintenance activities;
- the willingness to learn from maintenance-related events (successes and failures) including those involving external contractors; and
- the use of self-improvement teams (eg quality circles) and staff suggestion schemes to encourage staff to identify and implement improvements.

88 A strategy for maintenance improvement should include the following:

- continual re-appraisal of maintenance practices, including the views of maintenance staff and the analysis of plant- and equipment-reliability data;
- analysis of all instances of good and poor maintenance performance so that the underlying causes are properly understood (this includes incidents occurring during maintenance as well as incidents where poor maintenance was a contributory factor); and
- the sharing of ideas between the various maintenance groups/trades and the operations department, to develop and encourage good practices.

Further guidance is available in *Successful health and safety management*[1] and *Reducing error and influencing behaviour.*[5]

**Procedures and permits (contents)**

89 Maintenance procedures and permits-to-work provide important controls for ensuring high standards of performance and safety. The role of maintenance procedures is to provide sufficient information to allow the user to carry out tasks correctly, while permits and isolation certificates ensure that the appropriate safeguards are in place to allow the task to be carried out safely.

90 Maintenance tasks are generally very varied, with many tasks carried out only infrequently. Consequently, maintenance staff may need access to a comprehensive set of maintenance procedures to provide information on the required tasks. The level of detail required in the procedures will depend on the competence of the staff, the complexity of the task and how frequently it is carried out. There is also a need to have procedures to control critical maintenance activities, eg a permit-to-work system.

91 The reasons often quoted for staff not following maintenance procedures and permits are that they are perceived to be inaccurate, out-of-date, impractical, too time consuming, or that they do not describe the 'best' way of carrying out the work.

*A member of staff lost three fingertips while cleaning the blocked blades of a hopper. The hopper was accidentally started causing the blades to rotate. There was no automatic shut-off switch and the work was not being controlled through a permit system.*

*Guidance*

*Addressing the accuracy and practicality of procedures and permits*

92 Maintenance procedures need periodic review to ensure their relevance, accuracy and practicality. Such a review should be more frequent in situations where new procedures are regularly introduced or where changes are taking place such as the introduction of new technology. In particular, checks should be made to ensure that maintenance procedures and permits do not conflict with other requirements. They should not be too constraining, because if they are perceived to be overly restrictive or too severe they tend to be ignored. Conversely, it is important that the information they contain is not so general that it provides no specific requirements or practical guidance. Those people who will have to use procedures should have an input into their production.

*Determining when procedures are needed*

93 Maintenance procedures should only be specified to the level of detail required for an identifiable safety or quality need. They may not need to be detailed, or continually referred to, when the significance of an error is low in terms of safety or maintenance performance or the likelihood of an unrecoverable error is low. The likelihood of error is greater for more complex tasks, tasks carried out infrequently or where the competence of the staff is insufficient. Where the consequence of error is low, consideration should be given to providing a checklist rather than a full procedure. Checklists and job lists can also provide a supplement when using maintenance procedures for complex tasks. Simple rules can be used in situations where the consequence and likelihood of error are low.

*Content of procedures and permits*

94 Maintenance procedures, permits and rules should:

- be clearly and precisely expressed to avoid doubt;
- represent the best way of doing the job safely, without undesirable side effects;
- be limited in number, in cases where staff are expected to remember them accurately;
- be checked by staff to ensure they are practical, easy to follow, and fully understood;

- explain, where possible, the purpose of any controls and checks to enable staff to understand their importance, so reducing the risk of non-compliance; and

- ensure that the user can confirm that they have the most current version of the document (important if personal copies are held).

*Contractor procedures*

95 Care should be exercised concerning the adequacy of procedures used by contractors. They may not have the same familiarity with the systems and equipment as in-house staff. Where contractors use their own procedures, checks must be made to ensure that these fully reflect the standards and requirements of the organisation.

For further guidance on safety procedures see References.[5, 12]

**Procedures (presentation, understanding and usability)**

96 The complexity of many maintenance tasks requires that staff are provided with documentation to help them carry out their work safely and efficiently. To ensure that the documentation is followed correctly, it needs to be formatted and presented clearly. Mistakes are often made when procedures are not understandable or easy to use. This issue is particularly significant for maintenance because such mistakes are not always easily detected and corrected.

97 Procedures and other documentation only assist in ensuring high standards of safety and maintenance performance if they are used and followed correctly. Where the documentation is poorly formatted and presented, their use will be resisted by staff. The level of detail provided must suit the needs of the user and can vary from full procedures to checklists or job aids.

***Guidance***

*Clarity of text*

98 Text should be clear and unambiguous. Clarity concerns both the physical legibility of the text and the manner in which the information is presented. General guidelines include:

- Avoid using jargon as it can be misinterpreted, although industry standard terminology can be used where one is confident that all users will understand it.

- Use simple language.

- Avoid small text size or unusual fonts.

- Avoid unnecessary information which clutters the document.

- Ensure that the sequence of steps in the procedure reflects the actual maintenance sequence.
- Clearly highlight hazards, critical tasks and checks, eg with suitable warnings.
- Clearly indicate part numbers and other reference information, particularly where part numbers are very similar.
- Do not refer to other documents, unless strictly necessary.
- Any special tools required should be stated at the start of the procedure and not only at the step where they are required.
- Highlight unusual features of the task.
- Highlight any changes in the procedure.
- Use tick boxes to show stages in a sequence.

*Clarity of diagrams, illustrations and photographs*

99 Diagrams, illustrations and photographs are an essential part of many maintenance procedures. Care should be taken to determine the most appropriate type of illustration. This depends on the trade-off between a diagram, which can avoid unnecessary detail, and a photograph, which provides an accurate representation of the real system. When choosing illustrations the preferences of the maintenance staff should be considered. General guidelines are as follows:

- Use standard symbols and names to illustrate diagrams, etc taking care over using trade names and other non-standard terminology.
- Use the best orientation to show features, but ensure that the orientation remains compatible with actual viewing angles to avoid confusion.
- Use a size of diagram compatible with the amount of detail needing to be displayed.
- Avoid unnecessary detail but be careful not to omit critical details.

*Speed of access to relevant information*

100 The set of maintenance procedures needs to be structured to allow staff to easily find and access the information they require. This is particularly important for experienced staff who are likely to use procedures for reference only. When procedures are not routinely used for each job, arrangements are needed to inform staff of any changes. In addition:

- cross-referencing to different manuals should be minimised, and where it occurs it should be indexed;

- the indexing and cross-referencing systems should be clear and linked to tasks;

- use should be made of section breaks and physical methods, such as tabs, to allow the user to find the required section quickly; and

- procedures should be located as close as practicable to the workplace.

*Physical form of procedures*

101 Consideration must be given to the most appropriate media for procedures. Paper-based procedures must take account of the working environment, ie:

- working space, portability, dirt, weather and illumination, which may require procedures to be laminated; and

- ability to track progress through the document, eg it may be necessary to have checklists or tick lists.

102 Other media can be considered, eg computer-based procedures are easier to update and maintain but may not be accessible at the workplace. CD-ROM technology now facilitates the provision of significantly enhanced information, including sound and video clips. However, this must not be allowed to detract from the need to consider carefully the user's needs and how they can best be met. Users will not be helped by an enormous database of information if all they require is a simple checklist. *Reducing error and influencing behaviour*[5] provides further guidance on procedures.

**Work design**

103 When scheduling maintenance tasks, the workload of individuals needs to be controlled to avoid excessive stress or tiredness which can lead to poor maintenance performance. Although such issues are relevant for all tasks, it is often more difficult to plan the workload of maintenance staff who are often called upon to respond quickly to unexpected equipment breakdowns. Additional problems arise because maintenance tasks are often carried out during unsocial hours (eg nights and weekends). Equally, there is a need to avoid under-utilising staff as this induces boredom and a loss of skills, again leading to poor maintenance performance. High-hazard industries often make use of back-up systems to ensure safety systems are always available in the event of breakdowns. There is a need to stagger the maintenance of these systems. This will reduce the potential for individuals to repeat errors when maintaining a series of similar equipment. These errors could undermine the level of *redundancy* provided through the back-up systems by causing similar failures when they are required to operate.

104 Poor work design can have an adverse effect on job performance and occupational health, from factors such as excessive mental or physical stress (eg unrealistic timescales), excessive boredom (eg poor job variety) and lack of motivation (eg poor job satisfaction).

*Guidance*

105 Workload demands should be managed to suit the available resources and checks should be made to ensure that the workloads on specific individuals are acceptable. In addition, excessive overtime should be controlled. Not only can it lead to tiredness, promoting poor performance, but it can also lead to increased health risks from greater exposure to environmental factors such as noise and hand-arm vibration.

106 Tasks should be designed to reflect the physical and mental capabilities of the workforce. This can be challenging when the organisation is adopting multi-skilling strategies, because the competence of staff will vary. Equally important is the need to ensure that staff are provided with a broad range of work to maintain their competencies. Experience should be monitored to enable shortfalls to be identified and rectified.

107 Providing broad maintenance experience also has other benefits. It ensures job interest and may provide the opportunity for personal development. Work schedules which do not create adequate job variety can create problems in skill development or retention, particularly where multi-skilling is being introduced, and when staff are deployed to undertake unfamiliar tasks to cover for absences. Suitable variety, however, may prompt staff to be more conscientious about their work, so improving performance. Your organisation should be open to suggestions by staff on how to improve work design.

108 Tasks and maintenance schedules should take account of other relevant factors such as the interaction between maintenance and operational activities. For example, difficulties may arise if planning does not allow for situations where a significant proportion of maintenance work arises from breakdowns.

109 The design of maintenance schedules should also avoid the need for incomplete tasks to be handed over to another maintenance crew or shift, wherever possible. Care should be taken to avoid starting tasks too late in a shift for them to be completed, eg the task should be broken down into segments that can be completed within a shift, and checked and signed off before handover.

110 Tasks that cause single individuals to maintain a series of similar equipment increase the possibility of task errors being repeated, and should be avoided. This is of particular concern in high-hazard industries which make use of back-up safety systems.

***An electrician suffered severe burns while repairing a faulty 415-volt motor, which was live. Staff believed it had been isolated because the motor had been mechanically positioned for repair during the previous shift. However, there was poor communication across shifts and staff were unclear about who was responsible for isolating equipment.***

111 Where contractors are used, care should be taken to ensure that permanent staff maintain sufficient understanding of the tasks they undertake to provide proper control over contractors. Further guidance is available in *Reducing error and influencing behaviour.*[5]

**Crew/shift handover and shift work**

112 Where shift work is a part of maintenance, there are two consequential concerns. One is the potential errors caused by the shift-handover process. Failures in communication at crew or shift handovers are a common contributory factor to accidents associated with maintenance tasks carried out by multiple teams. Indeed, many of the UK's major accidents involve failures in the communication of key aspects of ongoing planned maintenance during shift handover.

113 Although there is an increasing move away from shift-based maintenance in many industries, some will always remain, either because of the nature of the particular industry or because of the need to support 24-hour operations with breakdown maintenance. Crew and shift handovers contribute to incidents particularly when safety systems have been over-ridden or there have been deviations from normal working practice, or the new crew/shift have been absent from work for a lengthy period. One key difficulty is that maintenance staff do not always recognise the importance of effective handovers especially where maintenance tasks are usually completed by a single crew or in a single shift.

114 Shift work often requires staff to work outside of normal waking hours. This can influence their sleep patterns and their performance. There are also the wider social impacts of shift rotas. Shift schedules which fail to take account of human limitation can adversely affect maintenance performance. Both shift periods and patterns need to be considered.

***Guidance***

*Crew and shift handovers*

115 To minimise the potential problems of shift/crew handovers, it is important to ensure that:

- handovers receive a high priority with the necessary resources provided (eg sufficient time),
- handovers of higher-risk maintenance activities are identified in advance and are subject to greater control (eg not subject to time pressures);
- guidance and training are provided to staff concerning effective handovers;
- handovers are seen to be a two-way process, with shared responsibility; and

- the information for communication during the handover is identified in advance and systems are provided to communicate it reliably, eg by using more than one form of communication (face-to-face, written log sheets, electronic records, etc).

*Shift working*

116 Shift working can often lead to problems and some of the guidance available is more concerned with minimising the adverse effects than with removing them. In either case careful management is needed. If this issue has been identified as a problem then it is also strongly recommended you read *Reducing error and influencing behaviour*[5] for more details. The guidance that follows is consistent with, and partly based on, this HSE guidance.

117 There are three key aspects:

- risks to health;
- possible impact on safety; and
- effects on shift workers' social and family lives.

118 Adverse health effects and severe fatigue resulting from poorly-planned shift systems (including excessive hours of work) can both lead to impaired performance and so to an increased likelihood of accidents.

119 In the first instance, the decision to have shift-based activities for maintenance work should be reviewed. Where this proves essential, consideration should be given to minimising the amount of routine work undertaken on a shift basis, while recognising the need to ensure proper co-ordination of shift and non-shift based work. In addition, the following factors should be considered:

*Sleep*

Ensure that staff get enough sleep and of sufficient quality between shifts, particularly where staff both work and rest within a confined area (eg offshore installations). Suitably planned rest days should also be provided. Regular rest periods of at least 48 hours are likely to be necessary for shift (particularly night) workers.

*Adjustment*

Research suggests that true adjustment to shift patterns rarely occurs. Three days can be required to change from day to night shifts and vice versa. Adjustment is helped by using appropriate lighting levels, eg night-time work areas should be well lit.

*Shift patterns*

Forward rotation of shift patterns is currently considered better than reverse rotation, with fixed shift patterns the best, but socially less acceptable. Changing shift patterns about once a week is likely to cause more difficulties than a faster or slower changing pattern. Twelve-hour shifts minimise the number of handovers, but may be associated with a marked decrease in alertness and performance in the last three to four hours of the shift (see below).

*Time-of-day effects*

These are difficult to quantify but it is known that job performance may be poorer on shift work, particularly on night shifts where work may also take longer to complete. In general the time of highest risk for fatigue-related accidents is between 2.00 and 5.00 am, the early hours of the morning.[5]

*Time-on-shift effects*

Performance tends to deteriorate significantly with excessive hours, particularly more than 12 hours at work, although significant effects can be experienced before this without good management, eg provision of adequate rest breaks and a good working environment, avoidance of monotonous or very repetitive tasks.

*Individual differences*

Individuals vary in terms of their suitability for shift work, and in the type of shift patterns that suit them best. Consider what flexibility you can offer.

120 The social factors which affect the acceptability of shift working should not be underestimated. Most shift workers choose to become shift workers and so can be considered to accept the social impact. However, it must be recognised that personal circumstances can change, but the financial inducements of shift work can inhibit the required move from shiftwork.

Further information on shift working and fatigue can be obtained from *Effective shift handover - a literature review*[11] and *Reducing error and influencing behaviour*.[5]

**Individual capabilities**

121 Maintenance tasks are often carried out by individuals working with little supervision. Consequently, the quality of maintenance is particularly sensitive to the care and attention taken by maintenance staff. The organisation needs to encourage those attitudes and behaviours in staff which are conducive to high maintenance standards.

122 Maintenance tasks comprise two main activities: manual manipulation of components; and decisions required during fault-finding or following maintenance inspections. The first gives rise to problems associated with the strength, reach and dexterity required to manipulate components. The second type of activity may cause problems connected with decision-making, often in complex situations, eg during fault-finding. All these factors should be taken into account when devising and implementing maintenance programmes.

***A gas fitter nearly caused an explosion by forgetting to cap a pipe after stopping repair work for the day. When the homeowner turned on the gas it escaped into the kitchen. Fortunately, the problem was detected before a dangerous concentration of gas had built up.***

*Guidance*

123 All people are prone to making errors and this is more likely when they are tired, under time pressure, or exposed to distractions and interruptions particularly when carrying out familiar tasks. Ideally the potential for errors should be removed through good design, eg of procedures and equipment. Where this is not practicable a number of other strategies can be adopted depending on the type of error, eg through improved work design. The types of error associated with maintenance staff are described below. They are also explained more fully in *Reducing error and influencing behaviour*:[5]

*Slips and memory lapses*

Slips and memory lapses (eg accidentally pressing the wrong button or missing out a step or steps in a task) usually occur in tasks which are so frequently carried out that they become 'automatic'. In general, it is not possible to eliminate these errors through instruction or training. The best approach to controlling these errors is through design, by eliminating the opportunity for making them, eg through interlock guards, and ensuring that components can only be fitted in the correct manner. Where this is not practicable, the plant or equipment should be designed, or arrangements put in place, to allow errors to be detected and corrected before any adverse consequences occur, eg by giving feedback of the results of an action or through post-maintenance testing.

*Mistakes*

Mistakes are situations where, despite a genuine attempt to comply with procedures, an error of judgement leads to an inappropriate *rule* being applied or a step in a procedure being done out of sequence. Mistakes associated with an incorrect intention, eg believing that a bolt should be torqued to a value which is incorrect and then proceeding to torque it to that value. It is possible to reduce such errors by improving the training and the quality of procedural documentation. However, as the action is completed successfully in the eyes of the individual concerned, it can be difficult to 'self-detect' the error without external assistance, eg improved supervision or independent checks. Mistakes can also occur in novel situations where the individual does not have set rules to apply, eg in diagnosing a particularly complex fault. These situations rarely occur, but when they do the likelihood of error is high. These errors can be reduced by improved technical and decision-making training, use of diagnostic aids and improved teamwork to allow staff to obtain the advice of others.

*Violation (non-compliance)*

Violation is a separate form of human failure that occurs when an individual or individuals deliberately contravene established and known rules. They are therefore fully aware of what they should do but, for some reason, consciously decide not to follow the organisation's approved working practices. Retraining staff in the correct practices cannot be the answer, as they already know what they should do. Violations are addressed by ensuring that staff do not perceive the benefits of non-compliance to be greater than any adverse consequences. This can be achieved by ensuring that staff:

- understand the importance and need for specific maintenance requirements, eg by training;
- understand the consequences of non-compliance for themselves and the quality of maintenance;
- have the resources (eg time and tools) to carry out the requirements;
- perceive that managers and supervisors place a higher priority on high standards of maintenance performance and safety than short-term operational demands;
- are suitably supervised to ensure that good practices are encouraged and poor practices are discouraged through an effective disciplinary process which is consistently and fairly applied; and
- have practical user-friendly maintenance procedures supplemented appropriately by checklists and job aids.

***A manufacturing company was fined £11 000 after a worker was burned by liquid ammonia. Three fitters were removing pipework from an ammonia storage tank. However, they had not received any training and did not know the hazards associated with the substance. One of the fitters was sprayed with ammonia, which penetrated their clothing causing severe burns.***

124 Further information on reducing violations can be obtained from *Improving compliance with safety procedures: reducing industrial violations.*[12]

**Competence (technical and interpersonal skills)**

125 As maintenance tasks are often very varied the experience and skills of maintenance staff are important factors in ensuring high standards of performance. This is even more so in organisations that adopt a multi-skilling strategy. In addition to the technical competencies staff also need to have good interpersonal skills encouraging teamwork and communication. Your organisation must be able to ensure that maintenance managers have the appropriate management skills. Staff should also have a general awareness of the causes of maintenance error.

126 Problems arise when staff are asked to carry out tasks which they are not technically competent to undertake. This is a particular problem in maintenance because tasks are often carried out by single individuals with little support from

others. Problems also occur where staff do not retain their competence through retraining and/or appropriate experience.

127 Defining and verifying the competence necessary to perform a maintenance task is not easy. Competence depends upon both the capability of an individual and the appropriateness of that capability to a specific job, which may include some novel aspect not covered in the basic training. Individuals involved in complex tasks, such as some fault diagnostics, are even more difficult to assess for competency. Competency therefore needs to be considered in the context of the range of jobs and not in absolute terms.

*Guidance*

128 Maintenance staff should have gained the necessary basic knowledge of hazards and working practices relevant to their industry. For example, offshore workers would need general industry knowledge on explosion risks and evacuation procedures. They would also possess general knowledge gained prior to their employment from education, previous training and pre-employment qualifications. Such basic knowledge and competency would be expected for many employees in that industry.

*Competency*

129 This basic competency needs to be developed to such a level that individuals can work in a competent manner on normal maintenance jobs. This level needs to incorporate the additional specific skills and abilities relating to working methods and the use of specific tools which are necessary for the majority of the maintenance jobs expected to be carried out. Interpersonal skills may be required. This knowledge and ability can be termed the 'desired-knowledge template' for the job. The competence of individuals needs to be assessed against this template.

130 Although an individual may be judged to be broadly competent based on this template, the next stage is to assess the capability of the individual to work in a competent manner on rarely-performed tasks, perhaps in non-typical situations. Unfortunately this is not always straightforward. Evidence that maintenance crews or individuals are working in a competent manner may be established by assessing how well they undertake specific tasks. Care needs to be taken not to assume that an individual is competent merely because the maintenance work was satisfactorily completed. This measure does not necessarily address whether the work was carried out in a safe manner or to the specified procedures. Conversely, evidence of poor maintenance work does not always imply incompetence. There may be other problems which have nothing to do with competence, training or support. A further measure of competence is an individual's appreciation of their own limitations or lack of facilities or resources to undertake a specific maintenance task.

131 A database of qualifications and work experience may be the initial approach. However, the assessment of competence must deal with competency in specific jobs and

under specific conditions. Maintenance managers need to allocate work to individuals so that their competence and experience are fostered. Where feasible, a structured approach should be adopted to ensure that there are sufficient opportunities to reinforce their training and to keep up to date with new developments in the industry. There is sometimes a tendency to assign particular tasks to the same people in the knowledge that they will perform well. This practice deprives other staff of the opportunity to broaden their experience. This can also affect staff motivation and personal development.

*Training*

132 A training programme should be in place which provides individuals with the necessary knowledge and abilities to deal with unusual, and perhaps unforeseen, maintenance demands. Training should fully take into account the actual equipment and working conditions under which the real jobs need to be performed. Training should also reflect any local working practices. Training should highlight potential hazards and emphasise the rationale underlying maintenance procedures. It is important to recognise the importance of career progression and hence provide some supervisory skills (eg interpersonal skills) which may be required in the future.

133 Some training in the causes of human error will help maintenance staff to reduce errors by making them more aware of those factors which can influence their own performance. Such awareness can also lead to better reporting of the causes of near misses and other issues of concern.

**Teamwork**

134 Maintenance staff may need to work in teams, particularly when maintaining larger items of plant and equipment. Therefore, it is important that maintenance staff have the ability to work well with a range of other people, providing mutual support and advice, particularly for new staff. Furthermore, maintenance tasks need to be co-ordinated with other activities (ie operational activities) so it is important that maintenance staff work effectively with the operations staff.

135 A distinctive characteristic of maintenance teams is that they are often temporary, comprising people from different maintenance disciplines (eg mechanical and electrical), who may not normally work together. Problems can arise in this case if the teams do not form effectively and quickly. Permanent maintenance teams can also be found, eg in shiftwork. Permanent teams typically have detailed knowledge of each other's strengths, weaknesses and capabilities. While this permits them to make allowances for each other, it can allow unauthorised working practices to develop. Teams can suffer when an 'outsider' joins, perhaps to cover for leave. That outsider may not understand some of the unwritten rules (or 'team culture') that the team has developed.

*Guidance*

136 It is important that each team develops common objectives and that there are effective systems in place to ensure that the necessary knowledge and expertise is shared within the team. This requires both team leadership and internal communications. Teams generally have a number of strengths, especially in complex problem-solving. However, such processes can also introduce weaknesses, for example 'group-think' where the views of dominant individuals become the combined view of the whole team. Where maintenance teams are commonly deployed, it is important to provide some suitable training in team behaviour along with guidance on necessary communications skills.

137 Ad hoc teams require well-developed procedures and instructions in order to achieve their objectives. These procedures or instructions must clearly indicate the objectives and tasks of the team. Team members may mistakenly make assumptions about the actions or competence of other team members, based on experience of other teams, or they may unwisely defer to another person's views. In addition, ad hoc teams can be easily influenced by dominant personalities.

138 A further issue for team effectiveness is the interaction with other teams and external staff. Maintenance activities must interact with and support normal operations. Steps must be taken to ensure that teams do not develop obstructive relationships, either consciously or unconsciously, to protect themselves against 'outsiders'. Such protection can take the form of particular practices, conventions or communication styles. It can also take the form of rejecting external criticism and suppressing internal criticism. In addition, teams can sometimes start to 'self-destruct' when team cohesiveness is lost and team members start to attack or criticise each other's performance. Therefore, it is important that management encourages teamwork by providing adequate resources for staff training and directs support to team leaders and team members. Time will also be needed for team-forming and development, eg team meetings.

**Supervisor effectiveness**

139 Supervisors have an important role in correcting poor working practices while encouraging good ones. This can be difficult for maintenance supervisors, since maintenance is often carried out with little direct supervision. Consequently, maintenance supervisors may need to take a wider role and encourage a culture among their staff which supports high maintenance standards.

140 The skills and abilities needed by supervisors are often underestimated by organisations, and supervisors may not be provided with the support and training necessary. Particular problems occur when supervisors are promoted from within a team which still sees them as a team player rather than a team leader.

141 For most maintenance staff, the supervisor is their immediate 'management' representative and as such maintenance standards are often governed by the lowest standards tolerated by the supervisor. In cost-conscious environments, there are

***A trainee electrician suffered flash burns while working on a 415-volt electrical motor. The trainee was supposed to be working under the direct supervision of an experienced member of staff. However, at the time of the accident the level of supervision was very limited. The company was fined £2000 plus costs.***

strong pressures on supervisors to improve productivity. In such circumstances supervisors may focus on meeting production targets and allow safety and maintenance standards to decline. Where this occurs over a long period staff and supervisors come to regard these lower standards as acceptable.

*Guidance*

*Improving the commitment of supervisors*

142 Managers need to ensure that supervisors are aware that their behaviour may be interpreted by their staff as demonstrating a low commitment to safety and/or quality. For example, if supervisors do not correct poor working practices staff will see this as implied approval of those practices. Therefore, supervisors have to be encouraged and supported to demonstrate continually their commitment to high standards. This can be assisted by making supervisors accountable for the safety and quality standards within their team. Supervisors need to be especially vigilant towards new maintenance staff to ensure that they are adopting the high standards of the group and managers need to check whether supervisors rigorously monitor staff and consistently take corrective action.

*Improving the skills and abilities of supervisors*

143 Managers need to ensure that supervisors have sufficient training and experience in the desired working practices to enable them to identify poor working methods. Such training can promote a consistent standard between different maintenance supervisors and their teams. Supervisors also need support and training in line-management skills in order that they can encourage and support high standards and good teamwork. Where possible, equipment should be designed in a manner that highlights poor practices, eg colour-coding of lifting equipment which would allow a supervisor to identify quickly whether equipment is within its inspection period.

*Reviewing supervisor performance*

144 Managers should formally review the performance of their supervisors to ensure that standards are being maintained. Such reviews can be supported by checks and audits carried out by fellow maintenance supervisors and other staff, eg from production. Such checks can be very effective in encouraging good practices throughout the organisation.

**Environmental factors**

145 Maintenance is more susceptible to environmental factors because the environment is rarely ideal for maintenance activities. Maintenance tasks are often carried out in the field rather than in dedicated maintenance areas. Consequently, maintenance staff can be exposed to a range of environmental factors which can affect their performance and increase the likelihood of human error and stress. These

include high or low ambient temperatures, high humidity and noise levels, and poor ventilation and lighting. Difficulties created by poor working environments can also increase the likelihood that errors are not detected, eg by hindering post-maintenance testing.

146 The use of appropriate personal protective equipment (PPE) can help to minimise the effects of many of these factors, although the PPE may in turn adversely affect task performance and needs to be assessed. If the environmental conditions are particularly onerous (eg very high ambient temperatures), there may be a need to limit the exposure time of individual workers.

***Guidance***

147 It is important that environmental factors are considered when developing maintenance procedures and practices. In particular, care should be taken to avoid environmental extremes or, where this is not possible, consideration should be given to providing additional resources (such as additional staff or time) when undertaking such tasks. Additionally, consideration should be given to the scheduling of maintenance work during plant down times in order to reduce the potential effects of noise and high ambient temperatures, eg on boiler inspections.

*Temperature*

148 High and low temperatures can have a direct effect on the performance of tasks requiring dexterity. For example, at temperatures of below 16°C dexterity can be adversely affected. At high temperatures the capacity for physical work reduces with the increasing risk of heat stress. This problem is increased with high relative humidities. The need to wear certain types of PPE can also increase problems of heat stress. The influences of temperature, therefore, need to be considered both in terms of the basic task demands (dexterity and physical workload) and the need for and implications of wearing PPE.

*Lighting*

149 The need for appropriate levels of task lighting is usually well recognised. However, the level of lighting is often more appropriate to operations rather than to maintenance. Where maintenance requires higher levels of lighting this has to be provided by the use of portable light sources which may be less effective at providing suitable shadow-free illumination. Provision of lighting for external maintenance work undertaken at night needs to be considered as well as the need for glare-free working environments. Guidance on suitable lighting levels is available in a range of publications, such as those published by the Illuminating Engineering Society (IES) and in HSE's *Lighting at work*.[13]

*Noise*

150 Noise levels can be a distraction for staff especially where tasks are carried out in close proximity to running equipment. Hearing protection can be provided for personal protection and/or to reduce the distraction. However, it must be recognised - and allowances made for the fact - that such protection can detract from staff hearing warning signals and can also interfere with necessary communication between maintenance staff, and between maintenance and operations staff.

*Personal protective equipment*

151 PPE is often essential to protect workers from hazards during maintenance tasks, such as excessive noise and chemicals. However, such PPE can be a hindrance in the performance of a task if not carefully selected, eg when working in restricted spaces. Where PPE has to be used, it should be suitable and the associated procedures and work should be designed to allow for the limitations it is likely to place on users. In addition, where PPE creates difficulties for staff there is an increased chance that it will not be used. Such problems can be overcome if staff are allowed to choose, from a range of suitable PPE, those items which they find most comfortable and practicable to wear. Senior managers need to set the correct example by routinely wearing PPE themselves when required. Their example has been shown to strongly influence the willingness of the workforce to comply with PPE requirements. HSE guidance on PPE is available.[14]

***A maintenance fitter lost the tip of a finger while trying to clean a cake-stamping machine. The design offered inadequate protection during routine maintenance. The company was fined £7000 plus costs.***

**Plant and equipment design**

152 It is important that plant and equipment are designed so that the required maintenance can be carried out reliably and safely. Many of the situations that can cause poor maintenance performance can be eliminated or alleviated by improved design. However, designers often give scant regard to the maintainability of plant and equipment. Common problems include components that are poorly labelled, not easily accessible and which can be fitted incorrectly (eg the wrong way round). An additional problem is that the positioning of plant and equipment may not provide sufficient working space for maintenance activities.

153 Poor design features are often easy to identify, but are often not corrected by designers, contributing to dissatisfaction among maintenance staff. Designers should take account of ergonomic and human factors and design for maintainability, eg frequently visited areas will need safe, suitable and permanent access provided.

*Guidance*

154 Checks should be made against the following undesirable features during the design or commissioning process:

- Components and lubrication points which are awkward or excessively time consuming to reach.

- Designs which allow components to be incorrectly fitted or assembled.

- Components which are poorly labelled, or difficult to identify.

- Working postures which are awkward or uncomfortable, or which provide insufficient space to conduct maintenance.

- Tasks requiring excessive physical effort (designers sometimes specify forces which greatly exceed that which could be applied by most workers: this causes 'improvised' methods to be used such as extension bars on the ends of spanners).

- Machinery noise levels which could interfere with communications or cause annoyance.

- Instrumentation or other information systems which are, or have been, unreliable and may be subsequently disregarded or actively suppressed by staff (this includes alarm systems which give frequent false alarms – see *Better alarm handling*[15]).

- Difficult or time-consuming maintenance or preparation work, where the latter can often take more time than the 'core' job itself. (This can lead to short cuts being taken if maintenance workers consider the risks to themselves, other people, or even to the machine itself, to be low, or where the time allowed for the job does not take proper account of the required preparation).

155 Designs which highlight poor maintenance practices are to be encouraged. It may be possible to design equipment to increase the visibility of any breaches in maintenance requirements such as lack of lubrication.

156 Further information can be obtained from the following articles: Corlett and Clarke's *The ergonomics of workspaces and machines - a design manual;* Mason's 'Improving plant and machinery maintainability'; Pheasant's *Ergonomics standards and guidelines for designers.* [16, 17, 18]

**Routine checking of maintenance performance**

157 By its nature, maintenance is made up of activities which are a mixture of routine and non-routine tasks. As such, maintenance errors can originate from various sources. Some errors can be identified and corrected during maintenance, while others may be identified subsequently during post-maintenance testing. However, some errors will remain undetected when the item returns to service.

158 Although measures of maintenance performance are often collected, such as length of operating periods between repairs, this information is rarely used to monitor overall maintenance performance. Therefore, maintenance managers often have few objective measures of maintenance performance other than maintenance costs. This situation is not helped if the responsibility for plant and equipment is seen to reside within the production department.

159 The performance of the maintenance department needs to be routinely checked to identify and correct poor maintenance practices and to identify areas for improvement. Possible indicators of maintenance performance include:

- efficiency measures (eg repair times);
- equipment-reliability measures (eg mean times between repairs); and
- safety measures (eg accident frequency rate during maintenance).

There may also be value in monitoring measures for staff morale (eg absenteeism). The measures chosen should be cost-effective to collect and analyse, and should also reflect the maintenance objectives of the organisation.

*Guidance*

160 Monitoring of maintenance performance should take two forms. Firstly, the performance of significant maintenance tasks should be monitored, in particular those tasks with the greatest likelihood of error, eg:

- highly repetitive tasks or long and detailed tasks where staff can lose track of which items have been completed;
- rarely-undertaken tasks where staff can forget certain task steps;
- tasks dependent on non-maintenance staff, eg operational tests on reinstatement; and
- tasks undertaken in poor environmental conditions leading to possible short cuts or changes in working practices.

Such tasks should be devised to allow appropriate monitoring at critical stages, eg prior to re-installation.

161 Secondly, the overall performance of the maintenance department should be monitored, so as to ensure that inappropriate habits are not developing. There is a range of indicators that can be monitored including the following:

- Frequency of error-causing conditions identified during workplace inspections, eg poor environmental conditions, poor procedures, and the use of incorrect tools.
- Frequency of incidents and near misses, eg frequency of return-to-service errors and frequency of 'wrong parts used'.

- Frequency of maintenance revisits due to maintenance errors, including those identified during post-maintenance testing.
- Mean time between repairs.
- Frequency of equipment failure attributable to human error during maintenance.
- Accident frequency rate.
- Percentage of maintenance which is preventative rather than breakdown.

162 In selecting indicators, a distinction should be made between 'upstream and downstream' measures. Downstream measures reflect actual failures (such as accident rates), whereas upstream measures (such as findings from workplace inspections and risk assessments) identify those factors likely to cause failures. Monitoring upstream indicators provides a more proactive approach to management.

163 A further category of indicator which could be monitored concerns personnel issues. Factors such as absenteeism and staff morale provide indirect indicators of factors affecting performance.

**Review maintenance performance**

164 The overall performance of the maintenance function needs to be periodically reviewed to ensure that it is meeting the requirements of your organisation and to identify opportunities for improvement in performance. These reviews allow your organisation to be proactive. They facilitate organisational learning, and should not be confused with routine monitoring, which covers day-to-day matters.

165 However, maintenance managers often do not carry out such reviews because of an inability to stand back from daily maintenance demands. This inhibits maintenance managers from identifying areas for improvement. Maintenance reviews also present difficulties, as the effects of poor maintenance performance are often either indirect (eg impacting on equipment reliability) or delayed (eg affecting rarely-used safety equipment).

166 Types of reviews that can be considered include:

- quality and safety audits;
- safety-culture surveys;
- benchmarking studies comparing maintenance performance in different organisations; and
- the approaches outlined in this publication.

*Guidance*

167 There are various approaches which can be used to review the performance of maintenance functions including:

- questionnaires and interviews with staff to utilise the extensive knowledge they have of the system and how it functions;
- incident reviews to analyse the underlying causes of previous events;
- workplace audits using experienced personnel to look for error-causing factors;
- task analysis to provide a detailed understanding of tasks that appear to be error prone, thereby assisting the identification of preventive measures;
- human reliability analysis to identify the likelihood of maintenance error and to assist in identifying cost-effective preventive measures; and
- hazard identification techniques such as failure modes and effect analysis (FMEA) or hazard and operability studies (HAZOP), including Human Factors HAZOP, to identify the effectiveness of controls over critical maintenance activities.

168 It is essential that there is a robust system in place for acting on the results of any reviews. Effort put into reviews may be wasted unless appropriate measures to improve performance are implemented. Failure to implement the necessary actions could lower staff morale.

## APPENDICES

Figures 9, 10, 11 and 12 in the appendices may be freely reproduced, except for advertising, endorsement or commercial purposes. Please acknowledge the source as HSE.

# APPENDIX 1 INCIDENT REVIEW

1 Figure 9 is a score sheet which lists the main underlying causes of incidents and shows how they are associated with each maintenance management issue affecting the performance of maintenance staff (see paragraph 39 of the main text). There are a number of approaches for ranking the relative importance of each issue from information on the underlying causes of incidents.

2 Three approaches are given in Table 4 that vary in sophistication. The 'higher' level approaches are more reliable, but arc only likely to be justified when there is a degree of uncertainty in the rankings obtained from the 'simple' approach.

**Table 4** Ranking maintenance issues from incident review

| Level | Approach |
|---|---|
| **Simple** | Rank importance of each issue according to the number of times it was found to contribute to an incident. |
| **Medium** | Weight each underlying cause according to its relative importance as a contributory factor to the incident (using Table 5). Then rank the issues based on the sum of this weighting for each issue. |
| **High** | Weight each underlying cause according to the severity of the incident and its importance as a contributory factor to the incident (using Table 6). Then rank the issues based on the sum of this weighting for each issue. |

COPY THIS PAGE

**Figure 9** Score sheet for underlying causes of maintenance-related incidents

| Management issue | Underlying causes | Score 1 | Score 2 |
|---|---|---|---|
| Policy | Maintenance policy unclear | | |
| | Policy gave inadequate support to safety or equipment reliability | | |
| | Policy not communicated to staff | | |
| | Policy not supported by actions of senior managers | | |
| Resource allocation | Inadequate system for work planning and prioritisation | | |
| | Inadequate provision of resources to achieve scheduled maintenance, eg people, parts, equipment and time | | |
| | Failure to schedule necessary maintenance due to resource constraints | | |
| | Inadequate system of recording and prioritising equipment defects | | |
| Roles, responsibilities, and accountabilities | Poorly-defined responsibilities for maintenance staff | | |
| | Responsibilities of maintenance staff unclear to them | | |
| | Poorly-defined responsibilities of non-maintenance staff | | |
| | Responsibilities of non-maintenance staff unclear to them | | |
| Formal communications | Inadequate system of informing staff about maintenance and safety requirements and priorities | | |
| | Inadequate system of team briefing to promote safety and reliability | | |
| | Inadequate system for staff to report maintenance problems | | |
| | Adequacy of communication channels not monitored or reinforced | | |
| Management of change | Lack of consideration given to changes in plant or organisation | | |
| | Poor planning of changes | | |
| | Procedures and training not updated to reflect changes | | |
| | Changes inadequately monitored | | |
| Organisational learning | Inadequate priority and resources to implement improvement actions | | |
| | Management show lack of visible commitment to improvement | | |
| | Staff uninvolved and uncommitted to improvements | | |
| | Lack of willingness to learn from national and international best practices | | |
| Procedures and permits (contents) | Procedures contain technical errors | | |
| | Procedures contain inadequate information on task requirements | | |
| | Permits-to-work not completed correctly | | |
| | Errors in procedures and permits not reported | | |
| Procedures (presentation/ understanding and usability) | Task misunderstood because format of procedures is poor | | |
| | Procedures incorrectly followed due to poor format | | |
| | Procedures not used because difficult to use | | |
| | Procedures not readily available at place of work | | |
| Work design | Job beyond physical capability of person | | |
| | Job routine and repetitive causing lack of attention | | |
| | Poor use of skills causing loss of competence | | |
| | Excessive tiredness because of excessive overtime | | |

Score 1 = Score for each underlying cause  Score 2 = Total of scores for each management issue

| Management issue | Underlying causes | Score | |
|---|---|---|---|
| | | 1 | 2 |
| Crew/shift handover and shift work | Inadequate exchange of verbal information during shift handover | | |
| | Errors or deficiencies in equipment records and logs | | |
| | Excessive tiredness because of poor shift patterns | | |
| | Allocation of intricate tasks to night shift rather than day shift | | |
| Individual capabilities | Lack of care or self-checking during task | | |
| | Failure to obtain assistance when required | | |
| | Failure to use required procedures, equipment or personal protective equipment (PPE) | | |
| | Failure to report maintenance problems or inspection/calibration results | | |
| Competence (technical and interpersonal skills) | Inadequate technical training for task | | |
| | Inadequate training in personnel skills, eg teamwork | | |
| | Inadequate training of supervisors in line-management skills | | |
| | Inadequate training of maintenance managers in leadership skills | | |
| Teamwork | Poor teamwork with temporary work teams | | |
| | Poor communication within and between teams | | |
| | Poor support from other team members (eg of same craft discipline) | | |
| | Team members not promoting good practices and not criticising poor ones | | |
| Supervisor effectiveness | Inadequate monitoring of work practices by supervisor | | |
| | Poor example set by supervisor | | |
| | Supervisor did not correct poor practices | | |
| | Supervisor did not encourage good practices | | |
| Environmental factors | Inadequate lighting or poor ventilation | | |
| | Excessive high or low working temperatures | | |
| | Excessive noise or vibration | | |
| | Inadequate provision of PPE | | |
| Plant and equipment design | Poor access to plant and equipment for maintenance | | |
| | Poor labelling of equipment/components or test/calibration points | | |
| | Poorly designed or maintained tools or calibration equipment, etc | | |
| | Poor plant and equipment maintainability, eg parts able to be fitted incorrectly | | |
| Routine checking of maintenance performance | Inadequate monitoring of safety-performance indicators | | |
| | Inadequate monitoring of equipment-reliability indicators | | |
| | Inadequate monitoring of maintenance, inspection and testing performance | | |
| | Inadequate monitoring of personnel performance, eg absenteeism | | |
| Review maintenance performance | Inadequate review of maintenance, inspection and testing performance | | |
| | Inadequate planned inspections of workplace practices and conditions | | |
| | Inadequate assessment of previous accidents and incidents | | |
| | Inadequate audit and review of maintenance practices | | |

Score 1 = Score for each underlying cause    Score 2 = Total of scores for each management issue

**Table 5** Rating underlying causes based on importance to accident/incident

| Importance of underlying cause: as a contributory factor to the accident/incident | Weighting score |
|---|---|
| Minor contribution | 1 |
| Medium contribution | 4 |
| Major contribution | 9 |

**Table 6** Rating underlying causes based on importance to and severity of incident

| Severity of incident[+] | Importance of underlying cause as a contributory factor to the incident | | |
|---|---|---|---|
| | Low | Medium | High |
| Minor | 1 | 2 | 3 |
| Medium | 2 | 4 | 6 |
| Major | 3 | 6 | 9 |

[+] Severity can be in terms of personnel or public safety, equipment reliability or maintenance efficiency depending on the issue of concern.

# APPENDIX 2: WORKFORCE QUESTIONNAIRE

1 This appendix provides a workforce questionnaire (Figure 10) to obtain the perceptions of staff about which factors most affect maintenance performance (see paragraphs 45-47 of the main text). The workforce are asked for their views on the impact that various issues have on a maintenance problem, using the four-point scale in Table 7. The maintenance problem is one selected from those identified in the Identification stage (see paragraphs 32-34) and is included in the space provided in the opening question of the questionnaire, ie 'What effect do you think the following have on [insert maintenance topic being assessed]?' A questionnaire is used for each maintenance issue identified.

2 Clearly, it will help greatly if the identified problem is made as specific as possible. For example it could be:

- What effect do you think the following have on 'equipment reliability during the maintenance of diesel generators?'

- What effect do you think the following have on 'safety of the public during maintenance of equipment in a (specified area of public access)?'

In both these examples the main concern (eg equipment reliability, maintenance efficiency or the safety of employees and the public) and the nature of the maintenance operation itself (eg routine or breakdown maintenance, location of maintenance work or equipment type being maintained) are both specified.

3 When collecting all the completed questionnaires from the workforce, the responses are weighted using the values given in Table 7. A workforce-questionnaire record sheet (Figure 11) is provided to collate the total weighted scores for each question. The relative importance of each issue affecting the performance of maintenance staff is then calculated by averaging scores for the two factors associated with that issue. For example, factors 1 and 2 relate to the issue of 'policy', and so on with two factors per issue (see Table 4).

**Table 7** Weighting system for workforce questionnaire responses

| Contribution | Questionnaire response column | Weighting score |
|---|---|---|
| No contribution | A | 0 |
| Small contribution | B | 1 |
| Medium contribution | C | 4 |
| Major contribution | D | 9 |

**Figure 10** Workforce questionnaire

How much do you think the listed factors contribute to the following identified maintenance problem: ______________________________?

Examples:

**Factor 4:** if you think that there is ample availability of time and manpower for this issue (or that this availability, whether adequate or not, is not relevant to the particular factor) then for **F4** tick box **A** (as it does not contribute to this problem).

**Factor 8:** if you think that it is quite difficult to report maintenance problems and that this contributes to the problem then for **F8** tick box **C** or **D** (makes a medium or major contribution to this issue).

| **No contribution**<br>**Small contribution**<br>**Medium contribution**<br>**Major contribution** | | A | B | C | D |
|---|---|---|---|---|---|
| F | **Factor:** | A | B | C | D |
| F1 | Priority the company gives to maintenance | | | | |
| F2 | Practicality of the company's approach to maintenance | | | | |
| F3 | The availability of tools, equipment or parts specified for certain jobs | | | | |
| F4 | Availability of time and manpower needed for some jobs | | | | |
| F5 | Uncertainty about your level of authority, responsibility or accountability | | | | |
| F6 | Uncertainty over shared authority, responsibilities and accountability between your department and other departments | | | | |
| F7 | Manner in which the requirements of the job are discussed with you | | | | |
| F8 | Ease of reporting maintenance problems | | | | |
| F9 | Manner in which changes are introduced in the company | | | | |
| F10 | How skills and experience are maintained and developed in the company | | | | |
| F11 | How we learn from others within the company | | | | |
| F12 | How we learn from other companies | | | | |
| F13 | Procedures that are needlessly too detailed or complicated | | | | |
| F14 | Procedures that contain technical errors | | | | |
| F15 | Clarity of instructions in procedures/manuals | | | | |
| F16 | Speed with which information can be found in procedures/manuals | | | | |
| F17 | Complexity of some jobs | | | | |
| F18 | Physical workload demands on the maintenance crews | | | | |

| No contribution<br>Small contribution<br>Medium contribution<br>Major contribution | | A | B | C | D |
|---|---|---|---|---|---|
| **F** | **Factor:** | **A** | **B** | **C** | **D** |
| F19 | Quality of information received at shift handovers | | | | |
| F20 | Time allocated to shift handovers | | | | |
| F21 | Commitment of some of your workmates to the job | | | | |
| F22 | Time pressure you feel you are under | | | | |
| F23 | Technical ability of your workmates | | | | |
| F24 | Experience and competence of your supervisor or manager | | | | |
| F25 | Ability of people here to work together in teams | | | | |
| F26 | Co-operation you get from other teams or other departments | | | | |
| F27 | Amount of monitoring by supervisors | | | | |
| F28 | Amount of experience and help offered by supervisors | | | | |
| F29 | Quality of the working environment (lighting, air quality, noise, etc) | | | | |
| F30 | Type and quality of personal protective equipment specified | | | | |
| F31 | Physical difficulty of doing the work | | | | |
| F32 | Design features which make it difficult to identify faults and replace components | | | | |
| F33 | Commitment to collecting information on maintenance problems, accidents/incidents and near misses | | | | |
| F34 | Commitment to act upon information from accidents/incidents and maintenance problems | | | | |
| F35 | Extent to which the company is committed to identifying maintenance problems and causes of accidents and near misses | | | | |
| F36 | How the company tackles the issues most needing improvement | | | | |

Please add any suggestions you may have for improving maintenance here

Thank you for completing the questionnaire

**Figure 11** Workforce-questionnaire record sheet
(See extract from completed questionnaire record sheet given in Figure 8 page 20)

| Maintenance management issue | Total score for each factor (weighted 4-point scale) | | Score for each issue (averaged score) |
|---|---|---|---|
| Policy | F1 | F2 | |
| Resource allocation | F3 | F4 | |
| Roles, responsibilities and accountabilities | F5 | F6 | |
| Formal communications | F7 | F8 | |
| Management of change | F9 | F10 | |
| Organisational learning | F11 | F12 | |
| Procedures and permits (contents) | F13 | F14 | |
| Procedures (presentation/ understanding and usability) | F15 | F16 | |
| Work design | F17 | F18 | |
| Crew shift handover and shift work | F19 | F20 | |
| Individual capabilities | F21 | F22 | |
| Competence (technical and interpersonal skills) | F23 | F24 | |
| Teamwork | F25 | F26 | |
| Supervisor effectiveness | F27 | F28 | |
| Environmental factors | F29 | F30 | |
| Plant and equipment design | F31 | F32 | |
| Routine checking of maintenance performance | F33 | F34 | |
| Review maintenance performance | F35 | F36 | |

# APPENDIX 3 RANKING PRIORITY ISSUES

1 Figure 12 provides a sheet to record the rankings for each issue affecting the performance of maintenance staff based on the scores from one or both of the two assessment approaches (see paragraph 49 of main text).

**Figure 12** Record sheet for ranking priority issues

| Issue | Incident review | | Workforce questionnaire | | Overall rank |
|---|---|---|---|---|---|
| | Score | Rank | Score | Rank | |
| Policy | | | | | |
| Resource allocation | | | | | |
| Roles, responsibilities and accountabilities | | | | | |
| Formal communications | | | | | |
| Management of change | | | | | |
| Organisational learning | | | | | |
| Procedures and permits (contents) | | | | | |
| Procedures presentation/understanding and usability) | | | | | |
| Work design | | | | | |
| Crew shift handover and shift work | | | | | |
| Individual capabilities | | | | | |
| Competence (technical and interpersonal skills) | | | | | |
| Teamwork | | | | | |
| Supervisor effectiveness | | | | | |
| Environmental factors | | | | | |
| Plant and equipment design | | | | | |
| Routine checking of maintenance performance | | | | | |
| Review maintenance performance | | | | | |

# APPENDIX 4 WORKED EXAMPLES FOR INCIDENT REVIEW



1 This appendix gives two worked examples of the incident review method to illustrate how information on the causes of maintenance incidents can be used to identify and prioritise areas for improvement.

## Incident 1: Chemical leak from storage tank

### *Summary*

2 Approximately 20 tonnes of liquid carbon dioxide leaked from a seal on an access door on a storage tank. The tank was being returned to service following a five-yearly inspection.

### *Description*

3 Prior to the five-yearly inspection of the storage tank maintenance instructions for the work were prepared, including one covering the return of the tank to service. In preparing the latter instruction the documentation provided by the manufacturer was consulted. It was not clear from this documentation what material should be used for the seal joint on the access door to the tank. As access-door joints on other $CO_2$ tanks on site had previously been successfully assembled with compressed asbestos fibre (CAF) material, this was specified in the maintenance instruction. As an additional precaution the maintenance engineer asked to be informed if a different jointing material was found to have been used upon removal of the door. This was confirmed to be the case when the tank was being prepared for the inspection.

4 Once inspection of the vessel was completed a job card was issued together with the maintenance instruction to return the tank to service. The maintenance instruction required a new access-door joint seal to be made from $^{1}/_{16}$ -inch-thick CAF, but no reference was made to the size or design of the seal. The original joint seal was of a particular size so as to positively locate against the inner surface of the ring of bolts securing the door. This design did not require the use of a jointing compound to locate the seal in position. However, a different maintenance team returned the tank to service and no job handover appeared to have taken place between the two teams. In addition, the original seal had been disposed of prior to the handover.

5 The seal joint was made to a design which the second maintenance team thought appropriate and matched the raised annulus (ring) on the seal face. They did not realise that this was a different design to the original seal joint. With this design it was necessary to hold the seal in place with jointing compound. After the door was refitted, a request was made by the supervisor to check the door for even seating with feeler gauges. This check was not stated in the maintenance instruction.

6 The tank was then pressure tested with the pressure held for two hours. During this time the maintenance instruction required the pressure gauge to be monitored. The first reading of 22.5 bar was taken from the gauge on the local panel, which had a badly cracked glass. It was found after the incident to have a stuck pointer, although it was stuck in a position which gave a plausible reading. There were no labels to indicate that the gauge was inoperable, despite the cracked glass. A second reading of 22.0 bar was taken from the other pressure gauge on top of the tank. Since these two gauges would be expected to display slightly different readings, maintenance staff did not suspect any leaks.

7 When the pressure test was completed, the tank was filled with $CO_2$. Later a leaking noise was heard emanating from the $CO_2$ tank and liquid and vapour were seen to be leaking from the seal of the door. The leak was caused because the joint seal was of the wrong design and had been disturbed when the door was shut.

*Underlying causes*

8 The completed form on the underlying causes of this incident is shown in Figure 13. The significance of each issue has been weighted, based on its importance to the incident, using the scoring system outlined in Appendix 1.

Figure 13 A completed score sheet for this incident

| Management issue | Underlying causes | Score 1 | Score 2 |
|---|---|---|---|
| Policy | Maintenance policy unclear | | |
| | Policy gave inadequate support to safety or equipment reliability | | |
| | Policy not communicated to staff | | |
| | Policy not supported by actions of senior managers | | |
| Resource allocation | Inadequate system for work planning and prioritisation | | |
| | Inadequate provision of resources to achieve scheduled maintenance, eg people, parts, equipment and time | 1 | 5 |
| | Failure to schedule necessary maintenance due to resource constraints | | |
| | Inadequate system of recording and prioritising equipment defects | 4 | |
| Roles, responsibilities, and accountabilities | Poorly-defined responsibilities for maintenance staff | | |
| | Responsibilities of maintenance staff unclear to them | | |
| | Poorly-defined responsibilities of non-maintenance staff | | |
| | Responsibilities of non-maintenance staff unclear to them | | |
| Formal communications | Inadequate system of informing staff about maintenance and safety requirements and priorities | | |
| | Inadequate system of team briefing to promote safety and reliability | 1 | 1 |
| | Inadequate system for staff to report maintenance problems | | |
| | Adequacy of communication channels not monitored or reinforced | | |
| Management of change | Lack of consideration given to changes in plant or organisation | | |
| | Poor planning of changes | | |
| | Procedures and training not updated to reflect changes | | |
| | Changes inadequately monitored | | |
| Organisational learning | Inadequate priority and resources to implement improvement actions | | |
| | Management show lack of visible commitment to improvement | | |
| | Staff uninvolved and uncommitted to improvements | | |
| | Lack of willingness to learn from national and international best practices | | |
| Procedures and permits (contents) | Procedures contain technical errors | | |
| | Procedures contain inadequate information on task requirements | 9 | 9 |
| | Permits-to-work not completed correctly | | |
| | Errors in procedures and permits not reported | | |
| Procedures (presentation/ understanding and usability) | Task misunderstood because format of procedures is poor | | |
| | Procedures incorrectly followed due to poor format | | |
| | Procedures not used because difficult to use | | |
| | Procedures not readily available at place of work | | |
| Work design | Job beyond physical capability of person | | |
| | Job routine and repetitive causing lack of attention | | |
| | Poor use of skills causing loss of competence | | |
| | Excessive tiredness because of excessive overtime | | |

Score 1 = Score for each underlying cause    Score 2 = Total of scores for each management issue

| Management issue | Underlying causes | Score 1 | Score 2 |
|---|---|---|---|
| Crew/shift handover and shift work | Inadequate exchange of verbal information during shift handover | 4 | 4 |
| | Errors or deficiencies in equipment records and logs | | |
| | Excessive tiredness because of poor shift patterns | | |
| | Allocation of intricate tasks to night shift rather than day shift | | |
| Individual capabilities | Lack of care or self-checking during task | | 1 |
| | Failure to obtain assistance when required | 1 | |
| | Failure to use required procedures, equipment or personal protective equipment (PPE) | | |
| | Failure to report maintenance problems or inspection/calibration results | | |
| Competence (technical and interpersonal skills) | Inadequate technical training for task | | |
| | Inadequate training in personnel skills, eg teamwork | | |
| | Inadequate training of supervisors in line-management skills | | |
| | Inadequate training of maintenance managers in leadership skills | | |
| Teamwork | Poor teamwork with temporary work teams | | 4 |
| | Poor communication within and between teams | 4 | |
| | Poor support from other team members (eg of same craft discipline) | | |
| | Team members not promoting good practices and not criticising poor ones | | |
| Supervisor effectiveness | Inadequate monitoring of work practices by supervisor | | |
| | Poor example set by supervisor | | |
| | Supervisor did not correct poor practices | | |
| | Supervisor did not encourage good practices | | |
| Environmental factors | Inadequate lighting or poor ventilation | | |
| | Excessive high or low working temperatures | | |
| | Excessive noise or vibration | | |
| | Inadequate provision of PPE | | |
| Plant and equipment design | Poor access to plant and equipment for maintenance | | 9 |
| | Poor labelling of equipment/components or test/calibration points | | |
| | Poorly designed or maintained tools or calibration equipment, etc | | |
| | Poor plant and equipment maintainability, eg parts able to be fitted incorrectly | 9 | |
| Routine checking of maintenance performance | Inadequate monitoring of safety-performance indicators | | |
| | Inadequate monitoring of equipment-reliability indicators | | |
| | Inadequate monitoring of maintenance, inspection and testing performance | | |
| | Inadequate monitoring of personnel performance, eg absenteeism | | |
| Review maintenance performance | Inadequate review of maintenance, inspection and testing performance | | 4 |
| | Inadequate planned inspections of workplace practices and conditions | 4 | |
| | Inadequate assessment of previous accidents and incidents | | |
| | Inadequate audit and review of maintenance practices | | |

Score 1 = Score for each underlying cause    Score 2 = Total of scores for each management issue

## Incident 2: Non-return valve fitted incorrectly

### *Summary*

9 During a scheduled test of the feed-water system for a boiler, no forward flow was obtained. It was subsequently found that a non-return valve had been inserted the wrong way round.

### *Description*

10 The removal and refitting of the non-return valve for inspection was judged to be a routine preventive maintenance task. In preparing the work instruction, no consideration was given to the consequences of the activity being inadequately carried out. It was assumed that the fitters would follow the standard practice of marking the components to identify their required orientation, prior to dismantling.

11 In the event, the fitter did not mark the direction of flow on the components prior to dismantling. Instead the fitter decided to rely on the flow direction arrow on the body of the valve to show the required orientation for refitting. They had expected the testing of the valve in the workshop to be a quick job, so allowing reinstallation of the valve that shift.

12 Unfortunately, there was a delay in getting the spares required for refitting the valve. Consequently, the task of refitting the valve passed to another fitter. No job handover appeared to have taken place between the two fitters. To help determine the correct orientation, the second fitter checked an adjacent valve in the pipeline. They judged that the 'inlet' referred to the inlet from the feed pump. Noting the flow direction arrow on the body of the non-return valve, they fitted the valve in what appeared to them to be the correct orientation. The maintenance instruction provided no schematic diagrams showing flow directions, and flow arrows were not marked on the pipework. As the 'inlet' referred to the inlet from the boiler, the non-return valve was refitted the wrong way round.

13 The fitter had limited knowledge of the pipe layout for this system. Little plant familiarisation was carried out because it was deemed too difficult to fully familiarise all fitters on all the plant they might be required to work on. The supervisor was aware of this lack of familiarisation, but took no specific action.

14 Following valve installation, no post maintenance testing was carried out; the maintenance engineer judged that this was not necessary because of the apparently straightforward nature of the task. They did not properly consider the consequences of the activity being inadequately carried out.

### *Underlying causes*

15 The completed form on the underlying causes of this incident is shown in Figure 14. The significance of each issue has been weighted based on its importance to the incident, using the scoring system outlined in Appendix 1.

# REFERENCES AND FURTHER INFORMATION


1 *Successful health and safety management* HSG65 HSE Books 1997 ISBN 0 7176 1276 7

2 Department of Transport *Investigation into the Clapham Junction railway accident* HMSO 1989 ISBN 0 10 108202 9

3 'Vehicle Accidents' *Health and Safety Bulletin* 1995 **238** 7 ISSN 1353 1638

4 *The costs of accidents at work* HSG96 HSE Books 1997 ISBN 0 7176 1343 7

5 *Reducing error and influencing behaviour* HSG48 HSE Books 1999 ISBN 0 7176 2452 8

6 *Guide to occupational health and safety management* BS 8800: 1996

7 Bolton W *Production planning and control* Longman Scientific and Technical 1994 ISBN 0 582 22820 4

8 Rosander A C *Deming's 14 points applied to services* ASQC Quality Press 1991 ISBN 0 8247 8517 7

9 *Business re-engineering and health and safety management: Best practice model* CRR 123/1996 HSE Books 1996 ISBN 0 7176 1302 X

10 *The safe isolation of plant and equipment* HSE Books 1997 ISBN 0 7176 0871 9

11 Lardner R *Effective shift handover: A literature review* OTO96 003 HSE (Offshore Safety Division) 1996

12 *Improving compliance with safety procedures: Reducing industrial violations* HSE Books 1995 ISBN 0 7176 0970 7

13 *Lighting at work* HSG38 HSE Books 1997 ISBN 0 7176 1232 5

14 *Personal protective equipment at work: Personal Protective Equipment at Work Regulations 1992. Guidance on regulations* L25 HSE Books 1992 ISBN 0 7176 0415 2

15 *Better alarm handling* CHIS6 HSE Books 2000 available on www.hse.gov.uk/pubns/chis6.pdf

16 Corlett E N and Clarke T S 'Chapter 6 Maintainability' *The ergonomics of workspaces and machines: A design manual* Taylor & Francis 1995 ISBN 0 7484 0320 5

17 Mason S 'Improving plant and machinery maintainability' *Applied Ergonomics* 1990 21 (1) 15-24 ISSN 0003 6870

18 Pheasant S *Ergonomics: Standards and guidelines for designers* British Standards 1987 ISBN 0 5801 5391 6

While every effort has been made to ensure the accuracy of the references listed in this publication, their future availability cannot be guaranteed.

HSE priced and free publications are available by mail order from HSE Books, PO Box 1999, Sudbury, Suffolk CO10 2WA. Tel: 01787 881165 Fax: 01787 313995. Website: www.hsebooks.co.uk

HSE priced publications are also available from good booksellers.

British Standards are available from BSI Customer Services, 389 Chiswick High Road, London W4 4AL. Tel: 0208 996 9001 Fax: 0208 996 7001.

The Stationery Office (formerly HMSO) publications are available from The Publications Centre, PO Box 276, London SW8 5DT. Tel: 0870 600 5522 Fax: 0870 600 5533. They are also available from bookshops.

For other enquiries ring HSE's InfoLine Tel: 08701 545500, or write to HSE's Information Centre, Broad Lane, Sheffield S3 7HQ. Website: www.hse.gov.uk

Printed and published by the Health and Safety Executive C80 07/00